The Probability of God

The Probability
of God

HUGH MONTEFIORE

SCM PRESS LTD

Montefiore, Hugh
  The probability of God.
  1. Creation   2. Evolution——Religious aspects
  ——Christianity
  I. Title
  231.7'65   BS651

  ISBN 0-334-02276-2

334 02276 2

First published 1985 by
SCM Press Ltd
26–30 Tottenham Road London N1 4BZ

Typeset by The Spartan Press, Lymington
and printed in Great Britain by
Richard Clay (The Chaucer Press) Ltd, Bungay, Suffolk

Contents

Preface

It is not unknown for a Bishop of Birmingham to write about science and religion. Edward Barnes published *Scientific Theory and Religion* in 1933, and his son recalls how he would come down to dinner with some remark such as that, having spent all his day in calculation, he had reached the conclusion that space had a negative curvature (J. Barnes, *Ahead of His Time*, (London 1979, p. 309).

However, times have changed for bishops as for others, and in order to write this book I had to take three months' sabbatical leave. I would like to thank all those who made this possible: Bishop Michael Whinney and all others who have had extra work to do in Birmingham during my absence, the Church Divinity School of the Pacific in Berkeley, California, for inviting me to be 'Bishop in Residence' and above all its Dean, Bill Pregnall and his wife Joye for their hospitality and friendship without which this book could not have been written.

I would like also to thank those who have read through my manuscript and made helpful comments, although I must remain responsible for all that is written. I would like to add a special word of gratitude to my wife Elisabeth who has not only given me encouragement and shown patience throughout the project, but who has also helped to ensure that the book is written in sufficiently simple terms to be readable by someone without expert knowledge.

St Thomas Day 1984   HUGH MONTEFIORE

I

The Possibility of
Natural Theology

Anyone who writes theology must submit himself to the judgment of theologians; and likewise those who write about the sciences to the scientists. Those who are foolhardy enough to write on the borderline of both disciplines have to run a double gauntlet. Bishops in the past have not fared well in this exercise. Thomas Huxley's famous response to the Bishop of Oxford at the meeting of the British Society for the Advancement of Science in 1860 was more distinguished for its scorn than for its scientific acumen: 'If . . . the question is put to me whether I would rather have a miserable ape for a grandfather, or a man highly endowed by nature and possessed of great means of influence and yet who employs those faculties and that influence for the mere purpose of introducing ridicule into a grave scientific discussion – I unhesitatingly affirm my preference for the ape.' It is said that when the Bishop of Worcester reported these proceedings later to his wife, she replied: 'Descended from the apes! My dear, let us hope that it is not true; but if it is, let us pray that it will not be generally known.'[1]

But it did become generally known, and as Samuel Wilberforce's reputation plummeted, so Darwinism (and later neo-Darwinism) rose higher in the ascendant. Whatever might be the views of theologians (who, for the most part accommodated themselves to Darwinism)[2] or of scientists (many of whom are in their private lives very religious people),[3] there has grown up in popular consciousness the feeling that the sciences were advancing as the church began to recede; and originating perhaps from clashes with Galileo, Copernicus and Darwin, there is now a general assumption that in religious matters science is at the very best neutral and at the worst deeply hostile to religion.

Lately perhaps there have been some signs of a change; but professional scientists who have written on evolution from a religious point of view have been known to fare even worse than Bishop Wilberforce. For example, Teilhard de Chardin's *Phenomen of Man* attracted great attention when it was first published,[4] but Sir Peter Medawar's review in *Mind* was even more savage than Huxley's off-the-cuff reply:

> Some reviewers hereabouts have called it the Book of the Year – one, the Book of the Century. Yet the greater part of it, I shall show, is nonsense, tricked out with a variety of tedious metaphysical conceits, and its author can be excused of dishonesty only on the grounds that before deceiving others he has taken great pains to deceive himself. *The Phenomenon of Man* cannot be read without a feeling of suffocation, a gasping and flailing around for sense. There is an argument in it, to be sure – a feeble argument, abominably expressed . . .[5]

To intrude into this difficult no-man's land is to lay oneself open to the charge of indulging in (to use Medawar's phrase) 'some obscure pious rant'.[6] Only a strong sense of compulsion forces me, as a bishop untrained in the natural sciences, to walk through this minefield.

Why do I do so? For many years I have been teaching and writing about Christian theology, whether on matters concerning the New Testament, or about dogmatic themes such as the doctrine of Christ. I have come to realize that, without the foundation of natural theology, such subjects carry little weight with any but the diminishing circle of church people. Jesus as a great human being still exerts fascination over many. But the gospel he brought was good news about God. He brought it to a world in which belief in God was as natural as belief in the reality of the world in which people lived. The situation in the West today in this secular century is very different. The assumptions of society are at best agnostic and at worst atheist. Religion is becoming privatized as a legitimate hobby for those who are so inclined, instead of being publicly endorsed as the prior assumption of society from which the whole of life finds its meaning and structure.

Why ever should anyone in this secular society be interested in Jesus as the Son of God without a prior conviction about the reality of God?

Belief in God comes about in many ways. This book is concerned with the intellectual grounds of such belief. I am not so foolish as to think that anyone actually makes an act of personal commitment to God because he becomes convinced of divine reality as a result of pondering the intellectual grounds of that belief. People are people, not thinking machines; and personal reasons predominate in accounting for their commitment to God. But unless there is a predisposition to believe, and unless there is a presumption that belief is a rational choice which has intellectual justification, the atmosphere will not be conducive to faith. The claims for belief in God cannot be confined to the revelation of one particular religion: they must be universal. In the words of William Temple's well known aphorism: 'Only if God is revealed in the rising of the sun in the sky, can He be revealed in the rising of a son of man from the dead.'[7]

The welfare of religion therefore requires the resurgence of a natural theology of God which can command widespread consent. Howard Root wrote in *Soundings* twenty years ago: 'What we have to face today is a divorce of natural theology from the mind and imagination of the most sensitive segments of our society';[8] and during the last quarter century this divorce has spread far more generally in society. As Root reminded us then, Ninian Smart had aptly called natural theology 'the sick man of Europe'.[9]

This malaise about natural theology will have met with approval in some quarters. Pascal's experience was that the God of the philosophers was far removed from the God of Abraham, Isaac and Jacob:[10] and this is something which will certainly require future investigation. Kierkegaad asserted that 'truth is subjectivity', and inveighed against the very idea of systematic theology.[11] While it is true that cold intellectual thinking can never bring anyone into a warm and personal relationship with

God, it is also true that, while a subjective commitment to God may be satisfying to the self, it lacks credibility to others unless it is shown that there are good reasons for the actual existence of the God to whom commitment has been given.

So I would assert; but not all would agree. When I showed my thesis to Don Cupitt, he was kind enough to reply by summarizing his own contrasting position in these terms:

The first thing to explain about God is that he is a god – i.e. a focus and source of value, and object of worship. To get the logic of God right, you have to start with the *religious* meaning of God, namely that he is a personal and social god, one who functions as our religious ideal and as the *telos* of our spiritual lives. And when we understand how the idea of God works in our lives and what kind of authority it should have, then the only question is, am *I* going to shape *my* life this way? The question of existence is eliminated: it's a mirage created by the illusions of realism. To believe in God is to commit yourself to framing your life project in certain categories. Faith is the *choice* of a way of life, a God-oriented life. To prove that faith rational, I do not argue that something cosmic exists, for that ontic way of thinking seems to me long obsolete. Instead I try to show the rationality of faith by spelling out what the life of faith involves and showing the meaning and the worth it gives to life. Thus Christianity is to me, as to the man in the street, a way of life; and rational in so far as it can be shown to be the *best* way. Its proof is practical, not the proof of logical demonstration, but the proof of testing in life.[12]

I am grateful to Don Cupitt for this forthright reaction to the thesis of this book. Many would call Cupitt's view-point atheistic, but he insists that this is to misrepresent his position. 'I'm neither a metaphysical theist, nor a metaphysical atheist, nor a metaphysical agnostic. I simply explain theism in purely religious terms. My god is just the my-God of the Psalter, etc.'[13] Cupitt, in his rejection of metaphysics and 'the system', seems to come near to the view-point of Kierkegaad. I have already indicated that the relationship of the God of the philosophers to the God of Abraham, Isaac and Jacob needs further investigation. Certainly they are not at first sight the same, although I would hold that one leads to the other. As William Temple wrote:

'Natural Theology ends with a hunger for that Divine Revelation which it began by excluding from its purview.'[14] My basic problem about Cupitt's viewpoint is that for me, and I believe for the man in the street for whom he claims to speak, the metaphysical problem still exists. I cannot evade it. Is God real or not? Is the religious enterprise simply a search for personal authenticity, or is it the disclosure of a meaning and purpose in the universe as a whole? The man in the street, to put the matter in a suitably crude way, wants to know, 'Is there anybody there at all?', or do we just have to make the best we can for ourselves in a universe which is in itself random and meaningless? It is in part to answer this question that this book has been written.

There are others for whom natural theology is forbidden territory because it purports to bring fallen humanity in too close touch with the majesty and transcendence of God. I have in my possession a pamphlet by Karl Barth entitled simply 'NEIN!'[15] Barth said 'No!' to natural theology because he believed that there is no point of contact between God and man other than the divine revelation in Jesus Christ. For him man can respond to the Word of God spoken to him in Christ, but in no other way. Natural theology means thinking about God in the natural world solely by the light of reason, and that for Barth was a cardinal error. When Karl Barth agreed to give the prestigious Gifford Lectures in Scotland on the subject of natural theology, he began with the words: 'I certainly see – with astonishment – that such a science as Lord Gifford had in mind does not exist . . .'[16] The influence of Barth has been pervasive in Reformed circles and beyond. 'The tradition of Calvin and Barth finds no place for a natural theology, not so much because God has not revealed himself in his creation, as because human minds, through their fallibility and sinfulness, cannot recognize the testimony of the creation to God and proceed rather to project idols of their own imagining which can only be misleading and a corruption of the truth of God.'[17]

I have never understood how God can be the God of all the earth unless there can be real points of contact with him in addition to the Word spoken in Christ. In any case, I come from a Jewish family, and the idea that non-Christians are so totally blind that they can have no authentic knowledge of God is to me not only obnoxious but also disproved by my earlier experience.

Nonetheless, the familiar discourse within the Christian church today is frequently fideist, speaking in a language of faith which seems to have little relevance to the ordinary workings of the world in which we live, and which makes sense only within the charmed circle of Christian believers. This has added to the marginalization of the church, against which I have taken up my pen to write this book. If God created the universe, then we would expect to see his footsteps within it in a way which can be generally recognized by the light of reason. Sir Alister Hardy's 'plea for theology to be more natural'[18] is to be warmly endorsed.

I am writing this book partly because of this deeply held conviction that natural theology *should* be reinstated. But the other part of my conviction is that natural theology *can* be reinstated in the world of today. The pages that follow are an initial attempt to do this. It will not be a natural theology in the old sense of the phrase, or at least in the way that the phrase used to be understood. There are no proofs of God. There are no valid deductive exercises of logic, the premises of which all must accept and which conclude that God must exist. As the title of this book implies, I am writing not about certainties but about probabilities. Personal faith in God involves personal choice, but decisions about intellectual belief require the balancing of probabilities. John Henry Newman has some wise things to say about probabilities:

> Logic . . . fails to represent adequately the sum-total of considerations by which an individual mind is determined in its judgment of things; even its most careful combinations made to bear on a conclusion want that steadiness of aim which is necessary for hitting it. As I said when I began, thought is too keen and manifold, its sources are too remote and hidden, its path too personal, delicate and circuitous, its subject matter too various and intricate, to admit of the trammels of any language, of whatever subtlety and of whatever compass. Nor is it any disparagement of the proper value of formal reasonings to speak thus of them. That they cannot proceed beyond probabilities is most readily allowed by those who use them most.[19]

If we proceed by way of probabilities, it will become necessary to look in turn at various aspects of the universe in which we live, and also at various insights into and experiences of the human condition. It will be argued that a convergence of factors from these different considerations makes it far more probable that God exists than the contrary. However the main thrust of what follows will be concerned with what used to be called 'the argument from design'. It will not, however, be offered as an 'argument', but rather as a series of considerations leading to a particular probability. The advances in the natural sciences over the last quarter century have been so great that it is now possible to ask with greater precision and knowledge whether the evolution of the universe as a whole, and the evolution of life on this planet make it probable that there is a design underlying them. In the course of this investigation, it will be necessary to bear in mind the objections of those (such as Kant and Hume) who have claimed that the very idea of an 'argument from design' is doomed from the outset. It will be necessary also to state the case in a way which scientists will find unobjectionable. This in itself is a formidable undertaking. It carries with it two main risks.

In the first place, it carries the danger from which I must protect myself, that I may seem to give the impression that an intellectual case for belief depends on the acceptance of the scientific arguments that follow. When I showed my thesis to Michael Goulder (a Birmingham theologian who has resigned his Orders in the Church of England because he has ceased to believe in God), he replied: 'The scientific arguments you produce would, if they held, be sufficient to convince every reasonable person. However, you put your neck on the block, because if the scientific community does not accept them as valid, then you are allowing that all reasonable men will be right to reject as false the only basis for belief.'[20]

The second risk concerns the nature of explanation. When I consulted Maurice Wiles about my project he responded warmly, but with this warning: 'The more detailed the scientific account that one gives, the more risk there seems to me that God is being brought in as an explanation in the same sense as other aspects of purely scientific explanation.'[21] While I am encouraged by Sir Alister Hardy's plea that 'natural theology must become more truly scientific'[22] and by Rupert Sheldrake's view that scientific explanation is distinct from a theistic interpretation of nature,[23] I suspect that Maurice Wiles' warning explains why scientists are usually so suspicious of theologians who trespass on their territory. Science very rightly refuses final answers; and solutions to problems which *seemed* final only a generation or so ago, are now seen to be not so much untrue as inadequate. (To me, as a non-scientist, the most vivid example of this tendency is the supersession of Euclidian geometry by Einsteinian theories of the space-time continuum, or classical measurement by quantum theory.) Scientific answers can never be more than proximate, and the scientific enterprise works by doubt; whereas theological answers are ultimate, and the theological enterprise works by faith. Theological explanation, however, is at a different level from scientific explanation. To put it crudely, theological explanation gives answers to 'Why?' questions whereas scientific explanation provides answers to 'How?' questions. But the question I wish to pose is whether answers to 'How' questions now suggest an answer to the 'Why' questions. But the theologian must appreciate that there are those who question the legitimacy of asking any 'Why' questions at all in this area.

Here I must declare myself, and say that I believe very strongly in the Principle of Sufficient Explanation. If I didn't, I would lose all faith in the power of reason to solve problems, and as a result I would lose all confidence in rational conduct or even in any rational thinking at all. It seems to me extraordinary that many who spend their lives exercising their minds on human problems or on the investigation of the natural world (people who may well call themselves rationalists) should state categorically that the mind has no right to ask 'Why' questions about the universe in which we live. To me this is a dogma every bit as objectionable as religious dogma appears to rationalists.

In what follows, it will be my aim to eschew all dogma, religious or scientific. Whether I shall succeed must be a matter to be decided by my critics.

2

The Beginning of Everything

Modern cosmological sciences have given us a picture of the size and age of the universe that is hard to imagine. Francis Crick in his recent book (about the same size as this one) uses a striking means to demonstrate these:[1]

> Perhaps the most vivid method is to compare time to the lines of print themselves. Let us make our entire book equal in length to the time from the start of the Cambrian to the present; that is, about 600 million years. Then each full page will represent roughly 3 million years, each line about ninety thousand years and each letter or small space about fifteen hundred years. The origin of the earth would be about seven books ago, and the origin of the universe (which has been dated only approximately) ten or so books before that. Almost the whole of recorded history would be covered by the last two or three letters of the book. If you now turn back the pages of the book, slowly reading *one letter at a time* – remember, each letter is fifteen hundred years – then this may convey to you something of the immense stretches of time we shall have to consider. On this scale the span of your own life would be less than the width of a comma . . .
>
> Though it is difficult to convey a vivid and precise impression of the age of the universe, to grasp its size is almost beyond human comprehension, however we try to express it. The main

stumbling block is the extreme emptiness of space; not merely the few atoms in between the stars but the immense distance from one star to another. The visible world close to us is cluttered with objects and our intuitive estimates of their distance depend mainly on various clues provided by their apparent size and their visual relationships. It is much more difficult to judge the distance of an unfamiliar object floating in the emptiness of the clear, blue sky. I once heard a Canadian radio interviewer say, when challenged, that he thought the moon 'was about the size of a balloon', though admittedly this was before the days of space travel. This is how two astronomers, Jastrow and Thompson try to describe, by analogy, the size and distance of objects in space:

> Let the sun be the size of an orange: on that scale the earth is a grain of sand circling in orbit around the sun at a distance of thirty feet; Jupiter, eleven times larger than the earth, is a cherry pip revolving at a distance of 200 feet or one city block from the sun. The galaxy on this scale is 100 billion oranges, each orange separated from its neighbour by an average distance of 1,000 miles.

Within this universe there are some 10 billion galaxies at least, and our own galaxy has some 100 billion stars. The currently observed universe is some billion, billion, billion cubic light years. It is hardly surprising that Crick criticizes organized religion for a lack of awe and wonder at the sheer size of the universe in which we live.[2] However, even with the limited knowledge about the universe which existed at the time when the sacred writings were composed, the psalmist wrote: 'When I consider your heavens, the work of your fingers, the moon and the stars which you have set in order, what is man that you should be mindful of him, or the son of man that you should care for him?' (Ps. 8.5). We must realize that the author, in so writing, had no conception of the hugeness of interstellar space.

According to what was until recently accepted scientific opinion, all this almost unimaginable vastness exploded from a mere point, a 'singularity', from the boundary of time and from the beginning of space beyond which there is neither time nor space. Calculations put the awesome explosion (the big bang) some 15 billion years ago. The arguments which make this hypothesis little short of compelling are partly theoretical and partly evidential. The Second Law of Thermodynamics gives expression to the truths that the universe becomes more and more disordered, that this process is irreversible, and that (in an infinitely large isolated system) the total entropy in a system never decreases (entropy quantifies disorder). Projected forwards, this points to the ultimate 'heat death' of the universe, when maximum disorder is achieved and the system has reached a state of dynamic equilibrium. Projected backwards, the universe is most likely to have had a beginning, since the state of thermodynamic equilibrium has manifestly not been reached. But when did the big bang take place? Einstein demonstrated that gravity, as it were, stretches space and time. Hubble showed that the galaxies are rushing apart from one another – he did this by the famous 'red shift', the slight distortion in the colour of galactic light which signifies their relative movement. It was already known that the stars and the planets were not collapsing into each other by the force of gravity because of the contrary effect of centrifugal force. But Hubble showed experimentally that the galaxies, far from collapsing into each other, were actually distancing themselves from each other. Another way of putting this would be to say that the space between them is becoming 'stretched' or expanded. The position has been summarized by P. C. Davies:

> The energy density in the universe . . . determines its total gravitating power. A high density universe exerts more gravity, and causes a more rapid deceleration of the expansion. If the density is greater than the critical value, then gravity beats the expansion and succeeds in reversing the cosmic motion to a catastrophic collapse. If the energy density of matter is very much greater than the critical value, then this reversal (followed by obliteration) occurs sooner. Conversely, if the density is very low, the gravitating power of the universe is small, and the expansion proceeds more or less unchecked. Unless the energy density of matter is exceedingly close to the critical value, the universe would either collapse back on itself or explode.
>
> The same balancing act can be viewed from the opposite point of view. For a given density of cosmic material, the universe has to explode from the creation event with a precisely

defined degree of vigour to achieve its present structure. If the bang is too small, the cosmic material merely falls back again after a brief dispersal, and crunches itself into oblivion. On the other hand, if the bang is too big, the fragments get blasted completely apart at high speed, and soon become isolated, unable to clump together into galaxies. In reality, the bang that occurred was of such exquisitely defined strength that the outcome lies precisely on the boundary between these two alternatives.[3]

Hubble's Constant provides the theoretical basis for the big bang which initiated the universe. There are two pieces of confirmatory evidence. The first is the relic of the vast heat produced by the initial explosion of the 'singularity' into the space-time continuum. The expansion of the universe has cooled this from an estimated billion, billion, billion degrees (attained during the first billion, billion, billion billionth of a second after the explosion) to its present three degrees above absolute zero. This residual heat bathes the whole universe and the amount measured corresponds to the amount which can be calculated by means of the proportion of helium to hydrogen in the universe. Only during the first five minutes after the big bang would conditions have been sufficiently hot for nuclear reactions to have taken place. 'Calculations predict that the final ratio of helium to hydrogen should be about twenty-five per cent by mass, which is very close to what is observed to be the relative abundancies of these two elements today. Hydrogen and helium together constitute over ninety nine per cent of the material in the universe.'[4]

An initial 'singularity' no longer commands the consent of all scientists, with the advent of a quantized version of relativity. Stephen Hawking of Cambridge, describing recently his work on the quantum size of the universe (which begins from the mathematical description of the universe and proceeds to determine what a typical universe ought to look like) suggested, on the assumption that ours is typical, that it ought to have no singularity or 'beginning of time', but rather a time of very high but not infinite density, a state to which the universe will precisely return after its present expansion phase is over, to repeat the cycle ad infinitum.[5] Others consider that the cosmological problem is still wide open and alternatives to the big bang should be seriously investigated.[6] The rival theory put forward by Bondi, Gold and Hoyle postulated the appearance of new matter within the universe as it expanded, appearing out of a new type of field which carries negative energy. (It is perhaps not to be overlooked that Bondi and Hoyle had announced themselves to be convinced atheists, and that the 'steady state' theory would have abolished conventional ideas of divine creation.) This theory was at one time popular but the discovery of the cosmic background heat radiation led to its rejection. The big bang theory holds the field, and while it will undoubtedly continue to be modified, it is hard to see how it will be supplanted.

Why was there an initial explosion? It is hard to give any answer because it is not possible to think clearly about a situation outside space and time. It would be easy for a theist to try to resolve the situation by declaring: 'God created the universe by bursting the singularity which gave rise to it.' To do this however would be to confuse secondary with primary causes. (In any case the word 'cause' implies an antecedent action in time, and so it could only be used in this context with an extended meaning.) It is not inconceivable that, if there is a natural explanation of the events which have taken place during the expansion of the universe, a similar type of natural explanation might be given of the situation which gave rise to the big bang.

In any case there are theologians who have maintained that the doctrine of creation has nothing at all to do with science and cosmology. O. R. Jones[7] quotes J. S. Whale: 'The Christian doctrine of creation does not arise from our interest in explaining the world or accounting for its "origin" at some approximately datable time in the cosmic past. The doctrine of creation "out of nothing" is not a scientific description of the time series. Here no scientific statements are possible.'[8] Whale was not alone. Gustaf Aulen wrote that 'faith in God as Creator is not a theory about the origin of the world through a "first Cause", etc. It has in reality nothing in common with a rational explanation of the universe.'[9] Bultmann expressed himself likewise: 'The doctrine of creation is not a speculative cosmology.'[10] These writers are correct in so far as it is not the task of religion to give scientific answers to scientific problems. But cosmology certainly has implications for religion. It is possible to have a cosmology that is in conflict with religion, and it is possible to have a cosmology that is consonant with Christian doctrine.

As a matter of fact there is no one biblical doctrine of creation. Genesis 1 speaks of God making heaven and earth when all was *tohu vabohu*, formless chaos (Gen. 1.1). The details of the story must not be pressed, because an ancient creation myth has been used to serve as a medium of revealing the Lordship of God from the beginning. But the form of creation here is different from, say, that of Isa. 48.12, where creation out of nothing is clearly expressed:

> Hear me, Jacob,
> And Israel, whom I called:
> I am He: I am the first,
> I am the last also.
> With my own hands I founded the earth,
> with my right hand I formed the expanse of sky;
> when I summoned them, they sprang into being.

This idea of creation must be clearly distinguished from emanation, which was typical of ancient Greek thought. Emanation implies a necessary process, while creation is dependent on a free act of will on the part of God, and provides a personal explanation to the mystery.

It is not clear, however, that the concept of the big bang necessarily implies creation out of nothing. Other possibilities have been put forward. It has been suggested that the energy/matter which came into being at the explosion of the 'singularity' is a 'disconnected fragment of spacetime'[11] formed in rather the same way as when a bubblelike structure in a tyre caused by a puncture may expand and seal itself off from the main tyre. It may be that space and time are a 'synthetic structure, made out of component bits'.[12] Beyond the big bang, according to this theory, the components out of which the space-time continuum is composed existed already, but not in space and time.

J. A. Wheeler calls these component bits 'pregeometry', and P. W. Atkins gives a more amplified description:

The flickering, fleeting emergence of an incipient universe can be visualized as an aimless, purposeless stumbling of points into a pattern. Among those vast numbers of chance efflorescences there are one or two (or a comparably small vast number) less likely and more complex clusters that constitute a two-dimensional universe. Many in that less likely vastness happen to assemble in a way that defines a two-dimensional state without time, and so are surface without duration. Others assemble, once again at hazard, into a true two-dimensional spacetime, with a line of space and a direction of time. But they still lack enough complexity for survival. They are no more likely to survive than a cluster of motes in a sunbeam that briefly and transitorily happen to form a sheet . . .

One-dimensional universes were improbable patterns of points. Two-dimensional universes were yet more improbable patterns of the same points into more complicated, richer yet insufficiently rich, relationships. Much less probable still is the chance clustering that leads to spacetime of three dimensions. But still this spacetime is too flimsy . . . Vast numbers of such three-dimensional universes come, by chance, and have gone back, through structural poverty, to dust again.

Then (whatever that means) by chance a clustering of the points stumbled into a pattern of such complexity that it corresponds to four dimensions; they were four dimensions of space and lacked time . . .

One of those patterns was four-dimensional spacetime. We know that in fact it did occur at least once. We may also suspect that it is continuing to occur outside our space and time; but our particular flutter of dust is the one with consequences for us. That particular fluctuation was the stumbling of the points into the pattern we discern as three dimensions of space and one of time. By chance . . .

We stand now at the eye of creation . . .[13]

Dr Atkins' notes alongside his text are of great interest here. One wonders what his authority is for saying: 'All the while and everywhere, the geometry of spacetime is crumbling and reforming, but it is taking place on so small a scale that we fail to notice it.' One wonders how it can be known if it be too small to notice. More importantly, he adds:

The picture I am giving here is vague because it is a speculation about the form that the final solution of the problem of creation will take. Whereas it is possible to be precise and, with luck, even lucid about an established concept (because there is

something to comprehend and then to convey) it is possible
only to be vague about events preceding the creation because
they have not been established quantitively. Nevertheless there
are reasons why it would be unkind to regard these remarks as
ludicrous and outside science. In the first place there must be
some mechanism for the creation and its coming about. What
we are attempting to express by these remarks is that there is
the *possibility* of accounting for the creation and the events
which preceded it. We shall only have achieved the goal though
when this possibility has been expressed quantitively. When
that has been done I suspect that its verbalization will be along
the lines sketched in these pages. In a sense it is merely a hunch,
but one consistent with the entire thrust of modern science.

Since Dr Atkins wrote those words, his 'hunch' has been
followed by several scientific theories and speculations quantitively expressed, to explain the origin of the universe. In order to
understand these, it is necessary to try to 'think back' to the very
earliest moment of the universe, back to a period of time so short
that it is impossible even to imagine. It can be described only by
mathematical symbols.

We know that we live in a world where matter is composed of
atoms, but during the first half million years it was too hot for
atoms to exist. Roughly speaking, the earlier we travel back in
time, the hotter it gets as the universe gets smaller (so long as we
don't go back to the very earliest moment of all); and the hotter it
gets, the more matter becomes split into ever smaller components. Between the first three minutes and the first half million
years, matter could exist only in the form of nuclei and free
unbonded electrons. Earlier still, between the first 100 micro-
seconds (10^{-4}) and the first three minutes, it was so hot that
even the former could not exist, and matter consisted of particles
and electrons; and earlier still – and here the period becomes so
short that it is strictly unimaginable – between the first three
trillionth of a second (10^{-12}) and the first hundred micro-
seconds (10^{-4}) matter could only exist in the form of
'quarks' and leptons' and 'quanta'. Around three trillionth of a
second from the beginning, the temperature was so high and the
heat was so great that it is reckoned that two of the four basic
forces in the universe would have merged. We are familiar with

the forces of gravity and electro-magnetism. There also exist the 'strong nuclear interaction' (which bonds together the nucleus of an atom) and 'the weak nuclear interaction'. Around this point in time it is reckoned that the 'weak nuclear interaction' and the electro-magnetic force would merge, leaving only three forces in being. If we go back earlier still, to 10^{-35} second (that is to say, decimal point followed by thirty-four noughts of a second!) from the beginning, it is reckoned that there would be only two basic forces, for apart from the force of gravity, the other three would have become identical.

It is almost impossible to imagine anything happening at so short a period after the beginning, but it has been calculated that there may have been at that point a dramatic change in the size of the universe. Since it is known that the universe is uniformly expanding, it seems easy to extrapolate backwards in time, with its heat and energy gradually increasing, until a 'singularity' is reached when space and time began, with the universe's energy and heat infinitely compacted to a point. But it now appears that this may not be a true picture of what happened. The rate of expansion may not always have been uniform. At 10^{-35} second there may have been a dramatic increase in the size of the universe.[14] If at this point a microcosm (for whatever reason) appeared in an unstable vacuum, there could have been a momentary period of enormous expansion, an increase of size from a size smaller than a proton to a size slightly larger than an orange in 10^{-35} seconds.

Immediately before this expansion it has been calculated that the microcosm would have uniformly expanded until it 'super-cooled'. This 'supercooling' period would have destroyed the initial symmetry of matter and anti-matter, and would account for the existence of a universe which contains a preponderance of matter.[15] It would have been this 'supercooling' that initiated the brief period of exponential expansion. An interesting aspect of this theory is that the breach of symmetry (which was the cause of matter preponderating over anti-matter) would have occurred differently in different regions of the microcosm which comprised the primordial cosmos. Each region would have formed an impenetrable 'domain', and our observable universe would have fitted deep inside a single domain. So there is the possibility that our observable universe is embedded in a much larger (but not infinite) region of space in which other (unobservable) universes may exist. The simplest – and therefore the preferable – form of this theory is that the original primordial microcosm arose from a 'singularity' and expanded uniformly until the period of 'super-cooling' and exponential expansion took place. A variant of this is that the universe began in a random chaotic state, and only those small regions which were hot and expanding would have undergone inflation which enabled the observable universe (and other comparable universes) to evolve.

A further variant envisages a situation which it is quite impossible to imagine! We have been led to think of the universe beginning with a 'singularity' in which space and time began. It has been suggested that we think of this event as a 'singularity' because we can only imagine the four dimensions of length, height, breadth and time. But if there are in fact eleven dimensions, what seems to us to be a singularity would look differently from the point of eleven dimensions. 'The idea is that what looks like a singularity in four dimensions may not be singular at all when viewed from eleven.'[16] (These eleven dimensions, it is suggested, can only properly exist under exceedingly hot conditions. Under conditions such as those under which we live they have become compacted so tightly that we are only aware of their presence as the waves which carry the four basic forces of the universe above.) Clearly according to this theory, the primordial universe would have had a history which went behind what seems to us a 'singularity'; but into that period we can never penetrate.

These theories leave the creation of the original microcosm unexplained, however small it was at this almost infinitesimal fraction of a second before everything began. Whether God created it out of nothing, or whether a scientific explanation can be given of its occurrence is a matter which we cannot decide. Naturally scientists look for a scientific explanation, while theists are concerned to examine ways in which such a theory can be compatible with the creative activity of God; and of course there remains the possibility that the appearance of the microcosm could be just a 'brute fact'.

In fact there are those who have speculated further, to reach back beyond 10^{-35} second to 10^{-43} second, which is known as Planck time, and which is thought to be the time when energies and temperature were so high there is only one single unified force within the universe, gravity being merged with the other remaining force. Such speculations, however, require a theory of 'quantum gravity' which does not in fact exist. It has been suggested that the microcosm (which comprised the primordial universe) arose as a random fluctuation. According to this theory the universe is an accident, a random fluctuation which has resulted in the creation of everything out of nothing. (This theory would seem to fit well with the kind of description of the universe's origin provided by Dr Atkins.) A variant of this theory conceives of the random appearance of particles each of which (because its energy and mass would be so great) would be a 'black hole', and the universe is an accidental aggregation of matter in a fluctuating vacuum which occurred as it were amid an elemental foam of black holes.

These attempts to penetrate the Planck time must remain mere speculation because of the absence of a theory of quantum gravity. It is not for theologians to attempt to settle what belongs to the realm of the sciences. It may be, however, that we have reached the boundaries of scientific investigation and theoretical knowledge.[17] If this is the case, the precise origin of the universe must remain forever shrouded in mystery, even though it is possible to trace its history to within an infinitesimal moment of time after its absolute beginning. It may be that there are some other universes besides our own existing in separate and unobservable domains. Why should not a God will to create other such universes if he so decides? There is no question of predestination here because we are beyond the limitations of time. He knows all that has happened and all that will happen.

There are, however, questions which still remain with us which lie beyond the frontiers of the sciences. Why do the laws of the universe exist which have enabled our observable universe to develop and evolve as it has? Even if these turn out to be the only possible laws that could exist, we may still ask why they exist. Why did the original microcosm appear, or why was there something which appears to us to have been a singularity, or why was there an elemental foam of black holes from which an accidental aggregation of matter arose, or why were there quantum fluctuations out of nothing at all? John Hick wrote about the existence of the world:

I believe that the existence of an eternal being, the uncreated creator of everything that exists other than himself, provides the only possible final stopping point for our 'Why?' questions. In the face of the space-time system as a whole we can still properly ask *why* it exists. The question makes sense because it has a possible answer – namely that it is produced by an ultimate uncreated creative power. But we cannot meaningfully ask why an unproduced producer exists, for no more ultimate reality is conceivable by reference to which such a being might be explained. Nothing could, in logic, be more ultimate than the eternal self-existent creator of everything other than himself.[18]

We may agree that it is not possible to ask *why* an unproduced producer exists (because his existence must be necessary); but it is certainly possible to ask *whether* he exists. Nonetheless Professor Hick's statement could easily be adapted to cover the latest theories about the origin of the universe:

I believe that the existence of an eternal being, the uncreated creator of everything that exists other than himself, provides the only possible final stopping point for our Why questions. In the face of the hypothesis of 'pregeometry', or a 'singularity' or what appears to be a 'singularity' or the existence of the original microcosm of the universe, or an 'elemental foam of black holes', we can still ask why these exist. The question makes sense because it has an ultimate answer – namely that they are produced by an ultimate creative power.

And so we return to what philosophers of religion call 'the cosmological argument'. I am not a philosopher, and it seems unlikely that I can throw any fresh light upon the argument, except perhaps to indicate as I have attempted above, that recent scientific theories about the creation of the universe do not interfere with the thrust of the argument. This may take several forms. Swinburne summarizes his form of it as follows:

There is quite a chance that, if there is a God, he will make something of the finitude and complexity of a universe. It is very unlikely that a universe could exist uncaused, but rather more likely that God would exist uncaused. The existence of the universe is strange and puzzling. It can be made comprehensible if we suppose that it is brought about by God. This supposition postulates a simpler beginning of explanation than does the supposition of the existence of an uncaused universe, and that is grounds for believing the former supposition is true.[19]

On this argument Keith Ward comments appreciatively as follows:

> He argues that theism is more likely than any rival supposition because it has high prior probability and great explanatory power. By the latter he means that God would be likely to make a world like this, so he makes the world probable; and that the world on its own is very unlikely, since it is so complex, finite and particular. By the former he basically means that God is the simplest possible hypothesis which could explain the world. He is one being, whose powers, being unlimited, are the simplest possible, and who explains absolutely everything. So no theory could explain things better, or be simpler. Naturally I am very sympathetic to this argument.[20]

Professor Ward does, however, raise three points of reservation. One concerns the wide use made by Swinburne of the idea of simplicity, another concerns the claim to inductive probability, and another questions whether God is better regarded as the ultimate 'brute fact' rather than a logically necessary being. I do not think that it would serve our purpose to enter at depth into the philosophical argument here. It would, however, be useful to explain what Swinburne means by the simplicity of God:

> Theism postulates a person of a very simple kind – a person who is essentially omnipotent, omniscient, and perfectly free and who is eternal, perhaps essentially so. Such a being will be a necessary being and will necessarily be an omnipresent spirit, creator of all things, and (given that moral judgments have truth-values) perfectly good. Theism is also intrinsically simple in a further respect. According to the theist, all explanation is reducible to personal explanation, in the sense that the operation and causal efficacy of the factors cited in scientific explanation is always explicable by the action of a person.[21]

And so for Swinburne, God is not only a stopping point for

argument but also a necessary being. Ward, however, explores more deeply into this meaning of God as 'necessary being' by relating it to his inmost nature of self-giving love:

> If and insofar as 'self-giving love' is an essential characterization of God, he must create some finite world. Though such a world will limit his being in certain ways, it will also extend it in other ways. The limitations will always be self-created and the Divine dependence upon the world will always be such that God wills it and could revoke it at any time, so that neither denigrates from the primacy and perfection of God.[22]

Philosophers will continue to argue about the adequacy of Swinburne's view about the simplicity of God, and whether the concept of God as a necessary, perfect being is coherent rather than self-contradictory. If both his points be ceded, then there can be little doubt that it is simpler to ascribe the creation of the universe (or the disconnected fragments which compose it or the space in which it is embedded) to the agency of God. Ward writes approvingly of Hume's dictum that 'we should seek an explanatory scheme for the world which will be the simplest, most coherent, adequate, elegant, consistent and fruitful.'[23] Clearly God, at the very least, provides a *possible* explanation of the universe. For many he provides a *probable* explanation. The cosmological argument, however, because it starts from premisses to which not all could assent (e.g. that God is a necessary being) can hardly stand on its own as *convincing* evidence of the existence of God. Nonetheless, taken in conjunction with other probabilities, it could greatly strengthen the case for his existence. We shall have to return to it later.

3

The Development of the Cosmos

In the previous chapter I have tried to discuss the relationship of the big bang to the way people believe God acted in creation. What happened immediately after the big bang? To someone like myself who is untrained in the natural sciences, it seems very wonderful that cosmologists should actually have been able to make the most detailed calculations reaching back to within 10^{-43} of a second after the big bang itself. Before that point, as we have seen, the heat of the primaeval fireball was too intense for scientific explanation according to our present state of knowledge; and in any case it would not be possible to get back to the event itself, because at the event there was neither space nor time. Within these constraints, a very great deal is known, as can be seen, for example, from Steven Weinberg's book *The First Three Minutes*.[1]

Here I find myself in a difficulty. In view of my own ignorance, anything that I write must necessarily be borrowed from other people, as in the preceding chapter. The contents of the rest of this chapter, in so far as they bear on the development of the universe, I have unashamedly borrowed from Professor Paul Davies' writings.[2] Of course many others have written about these matters (and I have used some of their writings where these have been useful), but I have found those of Professor Davies (although, as it may appear, I do not agree with all his conclusions) to be the most helpful for my purpose.

As a result of the very remarkable progress made in scientific knowledge, and especially in the realm of physics, a great deal is now known about the physical forces at work in the universe in which the human race finds itself living. Precise calculations can be made about matter in its smallest forms (hadrons and leptons) as well as in its largest conglomerations (stars, galaxies and constellations of galaxies). These calculations raise some very important matters concerning the possible parameters of life as we know it, and these matters in turn raise important questions about the possibility (or even the probability) of divine activity within or upon the process. I shall attempt later in this chapter to assess their significance.

Had the nature of things been different from what it is, we would not be living in the universe in which we now find ourselves. That is obvious from the outset. At the same time, cosmologists have calculated that there exists in our universe what looks from the human point of view like a whole array of the most amazing coincidences. These are some of them.

1. Distribution of gases in the early universe

The universe, it has already been noted, appears to show a remarkable uniformity in the distribution of matter from the big bang onwards. It was once thought that random fluctuations among this hot gaseous material would result in increased density in some areas, and reduced density in other areas; and that the force of gravitational attraction would, in the process of time, result in the denser areas contracting into galaxies, and the galaxies themselves agglomerating into clusters. The expansion of the universe would work against this tendency, since it would 'stretch' the areas where galaxies would form, making them less dense. It therefore seems as though the initial conditions from the big bang must have been such that the gas was initially distributed with just the right perturbations to ensure the development of galaxies, neither so strong that the galaxies would implode into themselves, nor so weak that they would not form at all. (It is possible that these random fluctuations may have been caused by processes in the very early history of the universe which are not sufficiently understood today.) Whether or not the fluctuations were there from the beginning, *the delicate balance in the distribution of matter necessary to produce galaxies seems very remarkable.*

2. Primitive dynamic equilibrium

It has already been noted that very close to the big bang there existed a state of dynamic equilibrium. How was this primaeval chaos dissipated? There is, as has also been remarked earlier, an even consistency in the distribution of matter in the universe. Any ironing out of anisotrophy would cause dissipation into heat. An anisotrophy of only one part in 10^{40} would result in too great heat for an even distribution of matter. If the universe were to attain its present temperatures (which, as we have seen, is necessary for the evolution of galaxies) the expansion rate near the big bang required a uniformity in all directions within one part in 10^{40}. Professor Paul Davies calls this 'another stunning example of "cosmic conspiracy"'.[3]

3. The heat of the universe

It has already been noted that the residual heat from the initial big bang which bathes the entire universe is 3 degrees above absolute zero. If it were much higher than its present value, it is unlikely that galaxies could have formed (whatever their origin might be) because the gravity of this radiation would have been greater than that of matter. On the other hand, the universe must not be too cold, or galaxies could not form; for had it been too cold, this would have meant that there would have been very little primaeval turbulence, and this would have inhibited the formation into galaxies: the primaeval matter would not have produced fluctuations which would have separated into conglomerations of gaseous material, the forerunners of the galaxies. *It is remarkable that the big bang occurred in such a way as to make possible the eventual formation of galaxies, with the consequent possibility of life on earth.*

4. The weight mass of neutrinos

Neutrinos are the most ubiquitous objects in the universe. They are small, elusive, electrically neutral. They interact so weakly with ordinary matter that the earth is completely transparent to them. It used to be thought that they were without mass, but recent experiments suggest that this is not the case. Their weight cannot be large (5×10^{-35}kg) but there are so many of them that their total weight is thought to be greater than the total mass of the billions of stars in the universe. If their weight were only just slightly more than it is (say, 5×10^{-34}kg instead of 5×10^{-35}kg), the result would be to increase the strength of gravity in the universe as a whole with the result that, instead of its present expansion, the universe would actually be contracting. It is remarkable that such a small change in the mass of this minute particle should be able to make such a vast difference to the whole shape of the universe. Nor is this the only effect of such a change. Because neutrinos tend to accumulate near the centre of galaxy clusters, a slight increase in weight would cause a larger drag than there is now on the rotating galaxies, and would bring about considerable disruption. *It is remarkable that, if a neutrino has weight it should be so finely tuned for the orderly expansion of the universe and for the rotation of galaxies and their clusters.*

5. The mass of the universe

Because of the expansion of the universe, light as it travels across the universe chases the receding galaxies. The more distant regions recede faster. As expansion very close in time to the big bang was very rapid, light from one point never reached some other parts of the universe, and as time slows with the deceleration of the rate of the universe's expansion, it never will catch up. It follows from this that there are some parts of the universe completely out of touch with other parts. Since the big bang was some 15 billion years ago, the 'horizon' at any one point is some 15 million light years away from an observer. The total number of charged particles in the observable universe is around 10^{80}. (This is the square of 10^{40}, a number which crops up more than once in cosmological calculations, e.g. the age of the universe in certain atomic or nuclear units.) If the mass of the universe were only slightly more than it is now (say 10^{85} instead of 10^{80}), the force of gravity acting within the universe as a whole would have resulted in its collapse long before intelligent life could have formed. On the other hand, if matter were less abundant, the force of gravity would not have been so great, and the expansion would have been greater, and it has been calculated that galaxies or stars could not have formed in their present abundance. This is because the density within concentrations of gas and matter would not have been so great, and gravity would not have been able to restrain matter as it receded with the expansion of the universe. The mass of the observable universe is such that there is a fine balance near the critical point between these two possibilities, and our universe is stable, with an orderly rate of expansion. E.g., two galaxies, say 30 million light years apart, recede from each other at about 500 km per second. *It is remarkable that the present structure of the universe should depend upon this fine balance.*

6. Neutron mass

It has been calculated that if the neutron mass were reduced by only 0.998 of its actual value, then the free protons mentioned below would decay into neutrons, and the result would be that there would probably be no hydrogen atoms at all! *It is remarkable that the existence of hydrogen atoms (and thus the whole universe as we know it) should depend on this fine adjustment.*

7. The relative weight of neutrons, protons and electrons

An atom consists of a nucleus surrounded by a cloud of lighter particles, electrons, which are bound to the nucleus by electric forces. The nucleus is composite, consisting of proton(s) and neutron(s), both about 1800 times heavier than electrons. The force which binds together proton and neutron is known as 'the strong interaction'. In addition there is a 'weak interaction' which manifests itself mostly in particle changes (e.g. in the conversion of a neutron into a proton).

An apparently chance correlation of constants has been discovered. In the first place, the strength of the 'weak interaction' is found to be related to the strength of gravity. In the second place the electron mass is only a little less than the mass difference between protons and neutrons.

The result of these two apparently accidental constants is the present balance of hydrogen and helium in the universe. Free protons combined with free neutrons in the very early moments of the universe to produce helium, and those free protons which did not fuse with neutrons became hydrogen. Had the ratio of neutrons to protons been larger, there would have been a lot of helium, but very little hydrogen. Hydrogen is the staple food of stars, providing the material which is processed into energy by their 'nuclear reactors' within their cores. (Helium stars could exist, but they would not last long before exploding or burning out.) Without the present abundance of hydrogen there would be no stable stars like the sun emitting energy, and there could be no water on a planet such as our earth: and there could be no life as we know it. *It is remarkable that the existence of stable stars and the possibility of life on earth should depend upon this apparently chance correlation of constants.*

8. Gravity and electromagnetism

If the force of gravity were very slightly weaker, or the force of electromagnetism very slightly stronger, the nature of the universe would be very different from what it is. All stars would be of the variety known as red dwarfs. (These stars are smaller and cooler than average.) Red dwarfs are believed not to be able to have planets. By contrast, if gravity and electromagnetism were slightly stronger than they are, all stars would be blue giants (large stars, from which heat energy escapes mainly by radiation). In either case, the universe would be very different from what it is. *It is remarkable that the fine balance between these two forces of nature seems to make it possible for stars like our sun to exist.*

9. The strong nuclear force

Since elements heavier than hydrogen or helium which are found in a natural state on this planet consist of debris from earlier stars, we do not find in the earth any elements with an average life shorter than the earth. That means that we have no natural elements heavier than uranium (which has 92 protons and neutrons). It is remarkable that if the strong nuclear force (that is, the force which binds together protons and neutrons, without which they would explode) were to be weaker than it is, there would not be so many chemical elements. It has been calculated, for example, that if the strong nuclear force were only half as strong as it is, an element such as iron with 26 protons and neutrons (or even carbon with six), would not be stable. If the strong nuclear force were a mere five per cent weaker, then a deuteron could hardly exist, and deuterium is an essential element for the nuclear process within a star. On the other hand, if the strong nuclear force were only a few per cent stronger than it is, this would have resulted in hydrogen being so explosive that little if any could have survived, and the universe would have consisted almost entirely of helium. *It is remark-*

able, again, that the possibility of a planet where life as we know it could evolve should depend upon the precise value of this further constant.

10. *The weak nuclear interaction*

Our earth contains many elements without which we cannot conceive life, and which are indeed vital for the maintenance of life on earth. In particular carbon is a crucial ingredient of all living systems. Where did these elements come from? Only hydrogen and helium formed in the first moments of the universe after the big bang, before the density decreased so as to prevent further fusion of protons and neutrons. However, when stars formed, nuclear reactions began to take place, and the heavier elements were synthesized inside stars by nuclear process. When a heavy star exhausts its supplies of nuclear fuel, the core may implode rapidly and shrink to nuclear densities. This releases huge gravitational energy as a result of which the surface area of the star explodes. The explosion of a supernova, creating enormous luminosity, may be observed from earth by telescope. The force of the explosion disperses the heavier elements into the area around the galaxy, and later when stars and planets form, they incorporate these debris into themselves. Life as we know it could only occur because of the death of an earlier generation of stars. The process leading to this explosion is dependent on the strength of the 'weak interaction'. *It seems remarkable that the possibility of a planet where life as we know it could evolve should depend upon the precise value of this particular constant.*

11. *Carbon*

The whole of our life system is based on carbon. It is the vital life-giving ingredient, without which no living system such as we know it today could have emerged. Carbon, as has been noticed, is produced in the interior of stars which have exploded as supernovae and whose debris has been incorporated into our planet. Carbon forms when most of a star has already been converted into helium. A nucleus of carbon has six protons and six neutrons, while a nucleus of helium has two of each. Whereas the collision of two helium nuclei takes place very easily in the hot interior of stars where particles are in a chaotic state, the production of a carbon nucleus is somewhat complicated. First two nuclei of helium have to collide to form a nucleus of beryllium (which is short-lived); and a third nucleus of helium has to collide with this very quickly. Fortunately, the best heat for this to take place efficiently is to be found in the shrinking core of a hot star; and fortunately the heat adjusts to prevent the newly formed carbon being synthesized into some other heavier element. Fortunately, too, there is an excited state of carbon at exactly the right state in the core to enhance the rate of reaction. *It is remarkable that all this can happen in the interior of hot stars in such a way as to bring about the manufacture of large supplies of carbon, which is vital for the evolution of life as we know it.*

The most recent theories concerning the origin of the cosmos can take us one step forward: they can explain how it was *possible* for some of these 'coincidences' to occur.[4] What they cannot do is to explain their actual occurrence. In the same way, the latest attempts at Grand Unified Theory (the objects of which is to relate together the fundamental forces of the cosmos) may be able to show how 'constants' came into being, but what they cannot do is to explain the actual 'constants' themselves which have made possible the emergence of life on this planet. We have already in the previous chapter noted the theory that, in the very earliest moments of the universe, during its very hot phase, there was an eleven dimensional space time which, as the universe cooled, developed into the four dimensions of our experience, with the remaining dimensions as it were compactified into the waves which carry the fundamental forces of the universe.[5] According to this theory, all the constants of nature may have been determined by this dimensional change.

How then can these apparent coincidences best be explained?

Brandon Carter, at a meeting of the International Astronomical Union held in Cracow in 1973 to mark the 500th centenary of Copernicus' birth, read a paper on 'Large Number Coincidences and the Anthropic Principle in Cosmology'.[6] In this paper he described three classes of theoretical prediction. The first is the kind that has a natural explanation. The second he described as 'prediction based on the weak anthropic principle'. This he explained as taking account of the fact that 'our location in the universe is *necessarily* privileged to the extent of being compatible as observers'.[7] The weak principle applies to those 'coincidences' which can be explained by the fact that we are observing them from planet earth at this particular epoch in the development of the cosmos. The coincidences would not obtain (or would be different) if we were observing from some other vantage point of the universe or in some other epoch. The fact that we are where we are now means that the 'coincidences' are what they are now. To take one example, life cannot evolve on this universe until after some 10 billion years there is a plentiful supply of carbon from exploding supernovae, and that cannot take place until in an expanding universe at least one generation of stars has passed through its life-cycle. Likewise there is an end-limit to the possibility of life as the sun cools. The fact that we observe where and when we do, places a *biological* constraint on the features of the *physical* world. The strong anthropic principle is somewhat different. It is not that we as observers at our place and time impose a constraint on what we can observe – but rather that our position as observers is the cause of the universe as it is, with all its coincidences which seem so extraordinary. Carter puts it thus: 'The Universe (and hence the fundamental parameters on which it depends) must be such as to admit the creation of observers within it at some stage. To paraphrase Descartes: "cogito ergo mundus talis est"'[8] (I think, therefore the world is such as it is.)

Stephen Hawking, in a paper read at the same symposium, fills out what Brandon Carter means:

One now has to face the question of why the Universe should be expanding at so nearly the critical rate to avoid collapse. It seems difficult to explain this in terms of processes in the early stages of the Universe because the differences would be so small at these epochs: a reduction in the rate of expansion by one part in 10^{12} at the time when the temperature of the Universe was 10^{10}°K would have resulted in the Universe starting to recollapse when its radius was only 1/3000 of the present value and the temperature was still 10000 degrees. The only 'explanation' we can offer is one based on a suggestion of Dicke (1961) and Carter (1970). The idea is that there are certain conditions which are necessary for the development of intelligent life: out of all conceivable universes, only in those in which these conditions occur will there be beings to observe the Universe. Thus our existence requires our Universe to have

certain properties. Among these properties would seem to be
the existence of gravitationally bound systems such as stars
and galaxies and a long enough time scale for biological
evolution to occur. If the Universe were expanding too slowly,
it would not have this second property, for it would recollapse
too soon. If it were expanding too fast, regions which had
slightly higher densities than the average or slightly lower rates
of expansion would still continue expanding indefinitely and
would not form bound systems. Thus it would seem that life is
possible only because the Universe is expanding at just the rate
required to avoid recollapse.

The conclusion is therefore that the isotropy of the Universe
and our existence are both results of the fact that the Universe
is expanding at just about the critical rate. Since we could not
observe the Universe to be different if we were not here, one
can say, in a sense, that the isotropy of the Universe is a
consequence of our existence.[9]

E. R. Harrison puts the same point when he writes: 'The clown in
Twelfth Night only said half the truth when he said "That that is
is." The full truth is "I that am am, hence that that is is."'[10]

Carr and Rees have criticized the anthropic principle on the
ground that it is based on 'what may transpire to an unduly
anthropocentric concept of an "observer"'. They go on to say,
however:

There is no doubt that nature does exhibit a number of
remarkable coincidences and these do warrant *some* explanation. The anthropic explanation is presently the only candidate
and it cannot be denied that the discovery of every extra
anthropic coincidence in some sense increases the *post hoc*
evidence for it.[11]

Elsewhere, however, Rees writes:

Clearly the anthropic principle cannot provide a scientific
explanation of the universe in the proper sense. At best it offers a
stop gap satisfaction of our curiosity regarding phenomena for
which we cannot yet provide a genuine physical explanation.[12]

In a recent discussion Rees held with Weinberg, it was suggested
that the constants which make life possible on earth were laid

down in the ultra-early Universe by exotic processes involving concepts as remote from everyday experience as eleven dimensional space, and it is these few constants which determine all of present-day chemistry and perhaps biology as well.[13] But Rees did not explain why these constants have the values that they do. Ernan McMullin calls in question whether the anthropic principle can rightly be called in any sense an 'explanation' of the universe:

In what sense *is* this an explanation? One might call upon the isotropy of the universe, its age and size, the magnitude of the basic constants, in a causal account of how life originated. This would be a hypothetical explanation of the conventional sort. But the order may not be reversed. Even if one can show that life could have originated *only* if these same causal conditions were fulfilled, so that the logical implication works in *both* directions, it would not be permissible to explain the causal conditions in terms of the effect. Even if lunar craters were to be caused only by meteorite impact, the lunar craters would not serve to explain *why* meteorites fall on the moon. The principle of observers in a universe may allow one to predict that the universe is isotropic. But when isotropy can be said to be only one among a large number of possible universe-states, and one goes on to ask why it (and not one of the other states) should be the case, one cannot invoke as explanation the presumably at least equally improbable presence in it of observers. The question is rather: why should the *joint* state, observers plus isotropy, have occurred in the first place?[14]

If the anthropic principle does not really explain the strange 'coincidences' I have mentioned earlier in this chapter, how can they be explained? There are various ways in which this could be done.

1. *The order in our universe is an improbable accident amid all but universal chaos.* The natural order (with the particular constants which are part of the order) has occurred by blind chance, as a result of almost incredibly rare fluctuations of molecules which have produced large areas of 'co-operation'. This suggestion was made some time ago,[15] before the probable age of the universe was known and in this form scientists no longer take it seriously. It has recently resurfaced in a new form. According to the inflationary model of the universe, our cosmos

fits within one of many domains of a much larger region of space which had a short period of exponential growth (10^{50}) immediately after its emergence. Its development is not accidental: it has been governed throughout by laws of nature.

2. *The Universe is infinite in extent, but only a part of it is ordered.* This explanation seems no more satisfactory than the first one. Naturally we cannot observe what lies beyond our 'horizon', and so there are parts of the universe about which we can observe nothing. But from the observations that we can make, there is no reason to think (whether or not other universes exist) that one part of our universe is ordered and the rest is not; nor can any satisfactory reason be given for such a state of affairs. If, for example, our constants were known to change from epoch to epoch, this might give some grounds for thinking that entirely different conditions obtain in our unobservable parts of the universe. But this is not the case.[16] On grounds of economy and simplicity, this explanation must be rejected.

3. *The universe exploded from a 'singularity' and it will recollapse, but in such a way that it will explode again and again with the same results as those which ensued fifteen billion years ago.* The 'crunch-bang' theory is attractive, and it may be true. But at the moment it is not known whether or not the universe is open (i.e. will expand for ever) or closed (because the effect of gravity will overcome the rate of expansion from the initial explosion). 'All we can say is that the real universe lies very close to the dividing line between open and closed.'[17] The theory of an oscillating universe is in any case hardly an explanation of the 'coincidences' noted above. On the contrary it seems to suggest that the same 'coincidences' will recur again later in another epoch of space-time.

4. *The universe exploded from a singularity, and it will recollapse into a singularity, from which it will explode again in a different form.* Once again, this option presumes a closed universe, about which scientists do not agree. If, however, we do live in a closed universe, then undoubtedly at some time the force of gravity will kill the present expansion of the universe and it will contract, perhaps into a singularity. Will it explode again? If so, will the resulting universe be quite different from the one which we know? Will the constants be different, so that stars and galaxies cannot form? Will the mass of matter be different so that

the present nice balance of gravity over expansion rate will no longer obtain? The answer is that we do not know. Theoretical calculations have been and will continue to be made, but they cannot be tested, and they may be superseded. There is, however, a difficulty greater than that of theoretical calculation. At a singularity time and space come to an end. We enter the complete unknown. The universe has, as it were, come to an end. We may suppose that there will be another explosion of another singularity, out of which another universe will form. But, while we may speculate, we cannot know the reason for the explosion which formed our universe, we cannot be certain whether there will be another. What can it mean to speak of a *future* universe coming into being out of a beyond in which there is no time? It is true that if there were an *infinite* number of explosions of a singularity such as ours, one universe would appear with all the 'coincidences' which we have noted in our own, but there can be no necessary reason known to man why these explosions should take place.

5. *There could be an ensemble of an infinite number of universes of which ours is one.* When I wrote to Professor Paul Davies about my difficulties over the anthropic principles about which I had first read in his writings in the *New Scientist*, he was kind enough to reply:

> You are correct, I believe, in saying that the anthropic principle does not *explain* the more remarkable features of the universe. It may, for example, account for why we are living *here* (rather than in some other region of the universe) or *now* (rather than in some other epoch), but otherwise one can only say that if things are not as they are, we should not be here to comment on it. Thus, life is apparently a very improbable accident (in the sense that the universe is an improbable accident in which life has inevitably formed) or contrived, the latter being an essentially theological explanation that most cosmologists would regard as a 'last resort'.
>
> On the other hand, if it should be established that the universe we observe is not the only one, but there exist 'other worlds' with widely varying conditions, then the anthropic principle *would* explain the observed features, for life (us) would have selected only that subset of available worlds which permit biology. . .[18]

The concept of an ensemble of universes is compatible with two of the previous explanations, for if our universe were to be recycled in a way in which each cycle is randomly different from the 'previous' one, there would give an ensemble of universes sequentially rather than concurrently. The idea of an ensemble has a particular scientific appeal. Brandon Carter, in the article already cited, made an important distinction between prediction and explanation:

> It is of course always philosophically possible – as a last resort, when no strong physical argument is available, to promote a *prediction* based on the strong anthropic principle to the status of an *explanation* by thinking in terms of a 'world ensemble'. By this I mean an ensemble of universes characterized by all conceivable combinations of initial conditions and fundamental constants (the distinction between these concepts, which is not clear cut, being that the former refer essentially to local and the latter to global features).

Is such a viewpoint theoretically possible? According to some recent theory, our universe may be within one of many domains (most of which would have to qualify for the title 'failed universes'), but *this number cannot be infinite*. If it *were* infinite, it would at first sight give a *scientific* basis to the strong anthropic principle. For if there were to be an infinite number of universes, there would necessarily be one which corresponded exactly to the universe in which we now find ourselves, with all the 'coincidences' which we can observe and which have made it possible for us to be present as observers. On the other hand, there is no valid reason why we should postulate such a state of affairs, in order to upgrade the anthropic principle into the status of scientific explanation. It seems improbable. We are here at the boundaries of knowledge. It is hardly scientific to postulate an infinite number of entities which we can never in principle observe nor have any knowledge of their existence. If there is a simpler interpretation of the anthropic principle than this, it is to be preferred.

6. *There is an infinite number of universes which coexist with each other, and a new universe comes into being whenever two possibilities are actualized.* According to the uncertainty principle, it is not possible to know both the location and speed of an

atom or electron. If one is known, then the other is in principle uncertain. Furthermore, the uncertainty is only resolved by the action of an observer. If one looks for the location, it can be found, but the speed is uncertain. If one looks for the speed, it can be found but location remains unpredictable. (This principle holds good for individual atoms or electrons: there is statistical certainty about both the location and speed of a stream of atoms or electrons.) The reason behind this seemingly bizarre theory is that matter in its elemental forms behaves partly as a particle and partly as a wave. Be that as it may, it remains true that in some way the observer is involved in the nature of reality at a fundamental level. When John Donne said 'No man is an island' he never thought that this phrase could apply to man's relationship with the fundamental building blocks of matter!

If we now turn to the idea of an infinite number of universes, the quantum theory can be utilized to make sense of this. I borrow here words written by Professor Paul Davies:

> In this theory *all possible* quantum worlds are actually realized, and coexist in parallel with each other. Thus, every time an electron faces two choices *both* alternatives occur, and the entire universe divides into two. Each universe is complete with inhabitants (whose brains and presumably minds have also bifurcated) each set of which believes that the electron has abruptly opted for one of the alternatives. The two universes are disconnected from each other in the sense that it is not possible to travel from the one to the other through ordinary space or time. They exist 'side by side' or 'in parallel' in some abstract sense. And because there are as many universes as there are quantum choices, every possible arrangement of matter and energy will occur somewhere among the infinite array of parallel worlds.[19]

This theory is a form of the weak anthropic principle, that observers select this universe from a vast number of alternatives. Like the previous explanation, it suffers from the defect that it multiplies an infinite number of universes which we can never in principle observe and about which we can never have any knowledge; and so it fails to be a good explanation on the grounds of economy. It suffers from the further drawback that it negates the need for any scientific explanation because all possibilities can be realized in one of these infinite number of universes! In any case, it is not, I understand, possible to apply the quantum theory to entities of larger than atomic size, although the subject of 'quantum gravity' seems to take up a lot of the attention of cosmologists, even if they cannot come up with any satisfactory theory about it.

We have now briefly surveyed some of the remarkable 'coincidences' that enable life to evolve on this planet, and we have also briefly considered some of the possible explanations of how these coincidences can exist. There is also the possibility that they may have been contrived by a Creator. Not all theologians would wish to opt for this possibility. Dr Arthur Peacocke, for example, seems to prefer the concept of a 'chance universe':

> Chance must now be regarded as, not only operating to elicit the potentialities of matter-energy-space-time not only over the spatial and temporal scale of our present universe, but also over the ensemble of possible universes, in which matter-energy-space-time might be replaced with new entities consistent with other values of the physical constants and acting, presumably, according to quite different physical laws than those we can ascertain in principle in this universe.[20]

Dr Peacocke believes that chance may be seen as the divinely appointed means whereby all the potentialities of the universe are to be explored, and that the time-scale and the range over which 'chance' is thought to operate must be extended from this universe to an ensemble of all possible universes. In this way 'chance' and randomness are transformed in the divine purpose into creative agents.

Even if it is possible to make theological sense out of the idea of an ensemble of universes for which there is and can be no evidence, this does not alter the status of this theory as a *scientific* explanation. While it provides a *scientific* explanation of one universe with a particular set of constants which makes possible human life, it does not seem to me satisfactory in so far as it postulates entities that can never in principle be known, and it is infinitely complex in so far as it postulates an infinite number of universes.

The question arises whether an explanation that involves the

Creator is not infinitely simpler. It is possible that the existence of the universe has a personal rather than scientific explanation. Scientists dislike this kind of explanation. Once one introduces a personal explanation – the universe is the way it is because God decided it would be the way it is – no further scientific explanation is possible. The scientific enterprise has come to a full stop. Naturally scientists object to this, especially because in the sad history of the relations between religion and science the church has all too often tried to close down scientific enquiry and even to suppress scientific truth. On the other hand, when we consider the creation of the universe from a 'singularity' and when we ponder the nature of the initial explosion and the constants of nature which seem to provide the laws under which the universe must operate, it seems probable that we have reached the boundary of scientific explanation.

I realize that in writing these words, I seem to be presupposing a very anthropocentric kind of universe, in which it is being suggested that the kind of universe in which we live has been brought into being so that life may develop within it, and so that from life *homo sapiens* may evolve. Brandon Carter began his famous paper on the anthropic principle with the words, particularly apposite for a Copernican centenary: 'Copernicus taught us the very sound principle that we must not assume gratuitously that we occupy a privileged *central* position in the Universe.'[21] When we think of the vastness of cosmic space, and the almost unimaginable periods of cosmic time, it is easy to understand why scientists, and cosmologists in particular, dislike the easy assumption that man does hold a central position in this universe. We shall be considering the matter in further detail in a later chapter. Here I shall only say that the emergence of human consciousness, the ability to survey and reason about the universe of which we form an insignificant part, the capacity for personal freedom and personal relationships and the ability to appreciate the values of truth, goodness and beauty – these do seem to me to provide good grounds for assigning to man a central and privileged place within this vast universe, despite its billions of stars and galaxies and enormous regions of interstellar space.

Towards the end of this book we evaluate together the various possibilities which the recent advances of scientific knowledge put before us. Here we are faced *either* with the possibility of a personal explanation of the universe – that it was created as it is by divine will and choice – or that it is a random event for which no other explanation can be given to all its strange coincidences, other than they appeared by chance. The latter explanation is given by Weinberg at the end of his book *The First Three Minutes*:

> Some cosmologists are philosophically attracted to the oscillating model, especially because, like the steady state model, it nicely avoids the problem of Genesis. It does however face one severe theoretical difficulty. In each cycle the ratio of photons to nuclear particles (or, more precisely, the entropy per nuclear particle) is slightly increased by a kind of friction (known as 'bulk viscosity') as the universe expands and contracts. As far as we know, the universe would then start each new cycle with a new, slightly larger ratio of photons to nuclear particles. Right now this ratio is large, but not infinite, so it is hard to see how the universe could have precisely experienced an infinite number of cycles.
>
> However, all these problems may be resolved, and whichever cosmological model proves correct, there is not much of comfort in any of this. It is almost irresistible for humans to believe that we have some special relation to the universe, that human life is not just a more-or-less farcical outcome of a chain of accidents reaching back to the first three minutes, but that we were somehow built in from the beginning. As I write this I happen to be in an airplane at 30,000 feet, flying over Wyoming en route home from San Francisco to Boston. Below, the earth looks very soft and comfortable – fluffy clouds here and there, snow turning pink as the sun sets, roads stretching straight across the country from one town to another. It is very hard to realize that this all is only just one part of an overwhelmingly hostile universe. It is even harder to realize that this present universe has evolved from an unspeakably unfamiliar early condition, and faces a future extinction of endless cold or intolerable heat. The more the universe seems comprehensible, the more it also seems pointless.[22]

Stephen Weinberg can find no comfort in the universe, only in the fruits of his research about the universe, itself cold comfort except for the elite who can engage in such research. I write these words near San Francisco at ground level, looking like Weinberg on to a comfortable earth. It seems to me that Weinberg's preoccupation with the 'first three minutes' has closed his mind to a less 'pointless' possibility. I mean the option of the personal explanation, the divine choice that the universe should explode from a singularity in the way that it has done, or perhaps the divine choice of the component parts of the universe outside space and time which produced an explosion of the kind that took place at the big bang. It is hard to judge this probability against the probability of a chance universe with all the 'coincidences' that have been mentioned. As Weinberg writes, some prefer a particular explanation of the 'anthropic principle' 'in order to avoid the problems of Genesis'. For them anything rather than the religious answer. Others, however, opt against such an explanation of the anthropic principle (with its implication that the universe arose by chance) precisely in order to choose in favour of the religious option provided by divine creation.

Where lies the balance of probabilities coldly assessed? On the one hand it is claimed by some that in an expanding universe organized energy can appear spontaneously, without the necessity for it being present at the outset. There is then no need to attribute the cosmic order either to the activity of a Deity or to the input of organization at the initial singularity. Now we not only have attributed the origin of matter to expanding space, but also the origin of its organization. This, however, does not explain everything. For example, a fundamental law such as gravity which orders the cosmic expansion still requires an explanation. There are some who would assert that the order that we have in the universe may turn out to be the only possible order which could exist. 'In the future it is possible that the constants of nature will not be regarded as inexplicable within our universe.'[23] Whether or not this turns out to be the case, it may properly be objected that laws which are *logically* consistent are not necessarily existent (any more than the claim that God is logically necessary makes him actually existent). A complete explanation of the laws of the universe still requires a simple and complete explanation.

That can be provided by personal explanation. It therefore seems to me to have greater probability than any other explanation. As Professor W. H. Thorpe has put it: 'One can say that the

"Argument from Design" has been brought back to a central position in our thought, from which it was banished by the theory of "evolution by natural selection" more than a century ago. There seems now to be justification for saying that from its first moments the universe was "ordered" – programmed, was in fact Cosmos, not Chaos.'[24] As we have seen, there is a possibility that the universe did begin not in an ordered way but in dynamic equilibrium – that is in chaos – but if so it was a chaos which was, in the divine knowledge, bound to transform itself into Cosmos; and so Professor Thorpe's point holds.

which are vital for the maintenance of life; nor had I asked myself how the appropriate conditions had been maintained over vast periods of time so as to make possible the long story of evolution which has culminated in *homo sapiens*. I had not concerned myself with such things – until I read Jim Lovelock's book entitled *Gaia*.[3]

It so happens that earlier I had interested myself in ecological matters, and I had tried to draw attention to some of the dangers which imperil the human race by our thoughtless use of raw materials and by our unheeding pollution of the environment.[4] It was impossible to become concerned about such matters without being made aware that species great and small intereact with one another, and that the so-called 'balance of nature' is maintained in this way. Rachel Carson's book *Silent Spring* had made a profound impact on me, as it had done on so many other people. I came to realize that a pesticide might seem beneficial because it destroys particular insects which wreak havoc on certain crops, but this toxic substance could have unlooked for effects elsewhere in the food chain, and that the destruction of one set of insects could result in a plague of other organisms with a worse result than if nothing had been done. It became clear that ecology, defined as 'that branch of biology which deals with organisms' relations to one another and to their surroundings', would become an increasingly important branch of knowledge for the future of the human race, and that, if human ecology may be defined as 'the study of interaction between persons and their environment', man would find that he would have to pay greater respect to the environment in which he lives if he is to prosper in the future. I had even chaired a group of the Church of England's Doctrine Commission which tried to assess the importance of ecology for our understanding of Christian doctrine and ethics.[5]

I forget where I first heard of Jim Lovelock's book. I think that it was probably in a review I had read in *The New Scientist*. His thesis is that 'the biosphere is a self-regulating entity with the capacity to keep our planet healthy by controlling the chemical and physical environment'.[6] It is common knowledge that living organisms interact and by this means provide the necessary checks for the maintenance of an ecological balance. It is just as well known that self-regulating systems can occur quite naturally in inorganic as well as organic nature. These systems can emerge and develop by chance, because the elements which compose them happen to be at hand, and the energy which powers them happens to be in sufficient abundance. For example, the depth of a lake may be kept constant by the level of water in a river which drains it. It would be possible to imagine such systems on a global scale, setting up natural cybernetic controls which would maintain those elements that are necessary for life in the right amounts.

Dr Lovelock's thesis is much more striking than this. He proposes that biotic material – living organisms – forms part of a cybernetic system which makes possible the emergence and continuance of life on Earth and its evolution over thousands of millions of years. Can this be true? I cannot be certain; but in what follows I shall borrow as shamelessly from his writings as I have done in the previous chapter from the writings of Professor Paul Davies.

I write these words at Berkeley, renowned for its temperate climate which varies little more than twenty degrees between winter and summer. The pleasant environment of the Bay Area makes the region a popular one in which to live, and indeed California is the scene of one of the greatest migrations in human history. Of course a vastly greater variation of temperature than the fluctuations of climate experienced in the Bay Area is compatible with the continuance of life on Earth. But still there are limits. A climate in which the sea froze or the oceans boiled throughout the planet would rightly be considered unfriendly to life!

The Earth began its separate existence in space some 4,500 million years ago. The evidence from sedimentary rocks suggests that life was established on Earth more than three thousand million years ago (although it may have existed long before that without leaving traces of its existence). Dr Lovelock writes: 'Subtle evidence from the ratio of different forms of oxygen atoms laid down in the rocks over the course of time strongly suggests that the climate has always been as it is now, except during glacial periods or near the beginning of life when it was somewhat warmer.'[7] He reminds us that the ice ages affected only those parts of the earth outside latitudes 45° north and 45° south, whereas 70% of the Earth's surface lies between these two altitudes.

At first sight this constant climate over thousands of millions of years may not strike us as all that remarkable. But when we realize that over this period the sun's output of heat has risen by 25–30%, then this constancy of climate throughout this very long epoch of time seems quite extraordinary. Dr Lovelock writes:

> The climate and the chemical properties of the Earth now and throughout its history seem always to have been optimal for life. For this to have happened by chance is as unlikely as to survive unscathed a drive blindfold through rush-hour traffic.[8]

Naturally scientists have been looking for a natural explanation for this strange phenomenon. It seems as though the original atmosphere of the Earth was blown away early in its existence. There is some disagreement about the composition of its second atmosphere, although all agree that gases released by volcanoes formed the oceans and the air. There are some who believe that the early atmosphere resembled that of Venus and Mars, and that it was composed mostly of water vapour, nitrogen and carbon dioxide. (This is because the oldest known rocks, formed in Greenland nearly 4 billion years ago, could only have formed in an atmosphere containing carbon dioxide.) A more traditional school holds that it resembled rather the atmosphere of the outer planets Jupiter and Saturn, and that it consisted mostly of methane and ammonia.[9] Those who assume that there was 10% abundance of carbon dioxide at the start of life (in contrast to the present 0.03%) attribute a constant temperature as the sun increased its strength to an abiological control mechanism operating through the weathering of exposed silicate rocks.[10] Those who hold that there was originally a far higher carbon dioxide (and water vapour) abundance give most weight to the effect of a change in albedo (the degree of whiteness on the planet which affects temperature by reflecting heat back into space; the present albedo of the planet is about 45%), together with the effect of the slowing down of the rotation of the Earth round the sun. The main problem concerning such explanations is that, while it can be shown that there was a temperature at the start of life similar to that in our present epoch, it is not easy to demonstrate satisfactorily that there would have been a constant climate throughout the process.[11]

I have no competence to assess these or similar explanations. I note that Dr Lovelock (who holds the more traditional view) deems them to be inadequate, and explains how the original atmosphere was modified by various processes. He does not believe that abiological controls would have been sufficient to give the required results. He holds that the present atmosphere of Earth, with its major deviations from what would have been expected on a lifeless planet, proclaims the existence of life on Earth. He suggests that the presence of life on Earth has profoundly modified the composition of the atmosphere while at the same time it has helped to maintain a consistent climate. He points out that (if the original atmosphere was mostly ammonia and methane) the biosphere would have 'consumed' methane gas, and only a small perturbation from normal would have drastic results. 'Overconsumption' of methane would have resulted in a fall of temperature of little over 2%, but the long-term effect of this would have been to produce a frozen planet inhospitable to life. On the other hand, a system of control which 'overcompensated' for the consumption of methane would have resulted in the temperature of the planet approaching boiling point, which would have been equally inhospitable to life. A sensing mechanism and a fine-tuning system of control seems to be required to obtain a constant climate. He suggests that heat might have been conserved by lighter coloured micro-organisms turning black (and affecting the albedo) and that a similar effect could have been produced by marine biota so as to prevent runaway conditions of over-heating.

These are matters for speculation. The fact remains that compared with what it was three and a half thousand million years ago, the composition of the atmosphere has altered profoundly (whatever view is taken about its original composition). Yet, despite the increase in the sun's luminosity of 25–30%, there has been a constant climate. This is a very fortunate 'accident' for the evolution of living organisms!

Dr Lovelock also makes clear that, if life was to be maintained from its early states, a continuing balance between acidity and an alkaline environment was required, and also a reliable supply of those trace elements needed for specific mechanisms and functions, to say nothing of the need to deal with toxic wastes. He comments:

The first appearance of oxygen in the air heralded an almost fatal catastrophe for early life. To have avoided by blind chance death from freezing or boiling, from starvation, acidity or grave metabolic disturbance, and finally from poisoning, seems too much to ask; but if the early biosphere was already evolving into more than just a catalogue of species and was assuming the capacity for planetary control, our survival through those hazardous times is less difficult to comprehend.[12]

The atmosphere not only evolved into its present composition but it has also maintained its present components. This has taken place through subtle and delicate reactions not only between different gases but also between gases on the one hand and the biosphere and the lithosphere on the other. Each of the main reactive gases which comprise our present atmosphere seems to perform a function for the optimum maintenance of life. Because these gases interact with one another, it is not easy to describe briefly the function of any one of them in maintaining these optimal conditions of life; but a brief summary follows, derived from Dr Lovelock's explanations.

Nitrogen (which forms 79% of the atmosphere) is its largest component. It emanates from denitrifying bacteria and other processes of living cells. It seems to perform three main functions in the atmosphere. It is a useful gas for the maintenance of the air's present density, and this assists a stable climate. Because it reacts slowly with other gases, it makes an excellent dilutent for oxygen, as too much oxygen in the air would be fatal for life. It also prevents an excess of nitrate in the oceans which would also be fatal for the organisms which live there. If there is an abundance of nitrogen in the air, there is as a result less nitrate in the sea. Too much nitrate in the sea would raise its salinity to a level inconsistent with living cells. Furthermore large concentrations of nitrate can be toxic (as overliberal use of artificial fertilizers with run-off into the water table is beginning to demonstrate).

Oxygen (21% of the atmosphere) is essential to life. Although not the largest constituent of the atmosphere, it is the most important. It is necessary for energy, enabling birds to fly, mammals to move and humans to think. In an oxydizing environment, an element takes up oxygen as when iron rusts. By contrast, in our reducing environment, an oxide compound sheds its oxygen, as when plants by photosynthesis take up carbon dioxide and release oxygen into the air. So oxygen is recycled through the atmosphere. It is needed for the lighting of fires. The present 21% is optimal for our use. But if this percentage were to rise a mere four points to 25% the result would be that fires, caused by lightning or arising spontaneously, would rage in our forests unchecked and could not be put out. 'At the present oxygen level fires do not start at more than 15% moisture content. At 25% oxygen even the damp twigs and grass of a rain forest would ignite.'[13] This would destroy tropical rain forests and arctic tundra alike. It is remarkable that the atmosphere has been maintained at this optimum amount of oxygen. The constancy of oxygen concentration suggests the presence of an active control system.

Carbon Dioxide comprises only 0.03% of the atmosphere. This gas, however, is essential for life, because when it is oxidized it releases the carbon on which life systems depend, as well as the oxygen of which it is also composed. The present amount of carbon dioxide in the atmosphere is mostly maintained by its reaction with sea water. The oceans contain nearly fifty times as much carbon dioxide as there is in the air. Nature requires that the present amount of carbon dioxide has a 'greenhouse' effect on the temperature of the planet. (Combustion of large quantities of carbon fuels by human agency has raised fears that we may indeed be initiating a process which may lead to the overheating of the planet.)

Methane gas is found in very small quantities in the atmosphere, only 10^{-4}%. But it is important because it can help to regulate the amount of oxygen that the atmosphere contains. It can have, it seems, a two-fold effect. On the one hand it produces oxygen by a complex process in what is called the stratosphere (which is that part of the atmosphere which extends from between seven and ten miles as far as forty miles above the Earth). On the other hand its more important function is to consume by oxidation considerable amounts of oxygen in the lower atmosphere, without which the oxygen content of the air would rise disastrously. (Methane also helps to clear polluting substances from those anaerobic (airless) zones from which it originates.)

Nitrous Oxide is found in even smaller quantities in the air, a mere 10^{-5}%. Its function is its capability of destroying ozone. Ozone is a gas formed from oxygen. At its present strength in the stratosphere it shields us from the more deadly effects of ultra-violet rays from the sun. And so it is essential for life. On the other hand, if these rays were completely cut off, this would cause illness on earth, and would affect the climate. Fine-tuning is needed.

Ammonia (10^{-8}% of the atmosphere) recycles sulphur from the sea into the atmosphere from which it can be taken and returned to the land.

Methyl Chloride (10^{-9}%), like nitrous oxide, can affect the formation of ozone in the atmosphere.

Methyl Iodide (10^{-10}%) conveys iodine, an essential trace element for life, back to the land via the air.

Helium, argon and neon comprise 1% of the atmosphere, but they are not included here, because they are inert, and certainly inorganic in origin. By contrast the reactive gases, which are essential for the continuance of life, help to keep the climate stable. But how are their present proportions as components of the atmosphere kept constant? Dr Lovelock suggests that this result is fine-tuned by the action of the biosphere itself.

The supply of oxygen, for example, illustrates this thesis. How was oxygen accumulated in the atmosphere in the first place? The main source has been believed to be the splitting of water molecules in the stratosphere. The hydrogen atoms (being very light) escape from the Earth's atmosphere into space, and the oxygen atoms which remain behind either bond in twos to become oxygen gas or in threes to become ozone. This source, however, would be insufficient to account for the accumulation of oxygen in the air, to say nothing about the loss of oxygen by reaction with reducing materials exposed by weathering, volcanic outgassing, etc. Some other principal source of oxygen seems to be needed, and this appears to be supplied by the burial in sedimentary rocks of a small proportion (0.1%) of the total carbon which green plants fix in their own tissues. This small proportion is the carbon swept down the rivers and buried in the oceans. The removal of each carbon atom in this way releases one additional oxygen molecule, and this has helped to accumulate oxygen in the air.

But how has the present 21% proportion of oxygen in the air been maintained in such a stable way? Oxygen produced through photosynthesis by plants and algae is used up by respiration in a comparatively short space of time. This recycling process cannot keep the desired balance. It used to be thought that there was a balance between the net gain as carbon is buried and the net loss from the reoxidation of reduced materials extruded from below the Earth's surface. This, however, is too rough and ready a process for the fine-tuning required to keep the proportion at 21%. A sensing mechanism with negative feedback seems to be required.

Dr Lovelock suggests that this is achieved through the interaction of oxygen with methane gas. This is a biological product. It is produced by the digestive processes of ruminant animals. Its principal source is bacterial fermentation in the anaerobic muds and sediments of river estuaries, wetlands, marshes and seabeds, where carbon burial takes place. Over a billion tons of methane gas seems to be produced in this way each year. This contributes, Dr Lovelock suggests, to the fine-tuning of our oxygen balance. If the oxygen content of the air became too high, an increased amount of methane released into the atmosphere would reduce it; and vice versa. 'It is an intriguing thought that without the assistance of these anaerobic microflora living in the stinking muds of the sea-beds, lakes and ponds, there might be no writing or reading of books. Without the methane they produce, oxygen would rise inexorably in concentration to a level at which any fire would be a holocaust and land life, apart from micro-flora in damp places, would be impossible.'[14]

If the atmosphere is to retain a fairly constant temperature, its carbon dioxide level needs to be regulated. We have already noted that this depends on its reaction with the oceans which contain nearly fifty times as much carbon dioxide as the air. In the long run equilibrium seems to be achieved through the action of the silicate and carbonate rocks of the ocean floor and of the Earth's crust. But once again this is a very rough and ready means of control, which works over a long period. Some swifter means of fine-tuning seems to be required to maintain equilibrium. This could be achieved through the release into the oceans of the enzyme carbonic anhydrase (present in most forms of life), or through the sinking into the ocean bed of carbon-bearing shells of marine biota, or through the break-up of soil and rocks by life forms. These speed the reaction between carbon dioxide, water and carbonate rocks.

The biosphere may also be responsible for the recycling of trace elements necessary for life. For example, small red algae which live attached to the large bladder rack on the sea shore may be responsible for the production of dimethyl sulphide which enables the sulphur link to be completed by conveying it from the sea back to the land via the atmosphere. Similarly large marine algae which produce methyl iodine may fulfil the same role for iodine, a trace element vital for mammals. Phosphorus is another necessary trace element, and it is possible that there is a similar biological explanation for the recycling of selenium of which phosphorus is composed.

The atmosphere is maintained in its present composition, and the climate is controlled through the complex ways in which its gases react. In this process the oceans play an important part. Because we live on land, it is easy for us to forget that the earth's surface consists mostly of sea. The oceans themselves have remained remarkably constant for the last three and a half thousand million years. Continents have drifted, the polar ice has frozen and melted, the ocean levels have risen and fallen; but the oceans themselves have remained remarkably stable throughout, and the total volume of water has been constant.[15] It is most probable that life began in the oceans.

Everybody knows that the sea is salty. In fact it contains 3.4% salt, 90% of which is composed of sodium chloride, common table salt. Where does all this salt come from? A great deal of it is accounted for by the vast amounts washed down (together with much else) by the rivers into the sea; 540 million tons a year, in fact. But this is not the only source of salt. It comes also from below, pushed up from the interior by soft rocks. Geological evidence can be used to show that ever since the oceans came into being and life began, the saltiness of the oceans has not altered much. If the total amount of salt washed into the oceans every eighty years equals the total amount of salt in the oceans themselves, clearly there must be some very efficient mechanism by which salt is removed from the sea.

Various theories have been put forward to account for this. Ways have been suggested in which inorganic processes could have operated to bring about the required balance. The problem is complex since two salts, sodium chloride and sodium magnesium, both separate into positive and negative ions in water, and some means is needed to withdraw both types of ions from the seas.

The suggestion has been made that salts were withdrawn from the oceans by forming huge deposits in isolated areas of ocean where evaporation occurs at a faster rate than inflow of water by rain or river, and where these deposits would eventually be buried by natural geological process. This, however, is only a very rough and ready means of achieving a balance. Large fluctuations in the salt content of the oceans would have been bound to occur over epochs of time if this were the only means of control.

Such fluctuations, however, would have been fatal to life. 'One of the lesser known requirements for a living cell is that, with rare exceptions, the salinity of either its internal fluids or its external environment must never for more than a few seconds exceed 6%.'[16] (The salinity of the sea would affect through osmosis the salinity of the living cell itself.) If the saltiness of the seas had risen from its present 3.4% only to 4%, life we are told would have evolved differently in the ocean from what is revealed in the fossil records. A chance alteration in the salinity of the sea which would cause it to rise above 6% for a very short time would have put an end to all life in the oceans. Some more sensitive mechanism for controlling the saltiness of the oceans is needed than this kind of inorganic process. 'It would appear,' writes Dr Michael Whitfield, 'that although relatively simple geochemical rules probably control the overall composition of the sea, the distribution of elements within the oceans depends on an intricate interweaving of the chemically and physically possible and the biologically useful.'[17] Dr Lovelock has suggested a biological mechanism whereby the saltiness of the sea is controlled.

In the sea there are millions and millions of one-celled zooplancton, which feed on the micro-flora of the oceans in the upper sunlit layer of the seas within a hundred metres of their surface. These zooplancton are in turn consumed by larger predators which feed off them. They include both coccolithopores with shells of calcium carbonate, and diatoms whose skeletal walls are made of silica. (Silicon is one of the most abundant elements on the face of the earth and it is the main constituent of sand.)

The effect of silicon debris on the sea bed may be of very great importance indeed. Ninety-nine per cent of the silica washed down by the rivers sinks to the bottom of the sea, building up beds of silicate where it is stored in the same kind of way as fossil fuels which are formed from the carbon of the coccoliths. If increasing amounts of silica are washed down by the rivers into the sea, the diatoms will increase in numbers, and this would reduce the silica level at the bottom of the oceans. But if the amount of silica washed down into the sea diminished, the diatom population would decrease and less silica would sink to the seabed. The silica falling to the seabed with the rest of the debris sinking to the sea-floor would trap salt washed down by the rivers of the world and remove it from the sea. This biological mechanism could provide the fine tuning required to even out irregularities involved if regulation were merely by inorganic process. Dr Lovelock has even suggested the possibility of a biological control at work in regulating the amount of salts extruded into the oceans from below the earth's crust. The deposits of silica on the ocean bed would act as a kind of muffler, heating up the areas beneath the sedimentary rocks, and the weight of these silicate deposits would press down on the crust until there was a violent reaction in the form of a submarine volcanic eruption.

These speculations are only hypotheses. It may be that they can be disproved by further research or modified by other scientific ideas. They seemed to me so extraordinary that I did not know whether or not to take them seriously. I noticed that Jim Lovelock is a Fellow of the Royal Society and that his book was published by the Oxford University Press. That seemed respectable enough. I tried to find out how Dr Lovelock's theories have been received. 'Lovelock's hypothesis is regarded with suspicion by most scientists' reported John Gribbin.[18] What did Dr Lovelock himself think? 'The Gaia hypothesis has tended to be ignored rather than criticized by geochemists,' he writes, 'almost as if Aristotle still ruled, and anything moving towards a circular, even a non-linear argument is forbidden. Gaia which uses the circular reasoning of cybernetics was taken to be teleological.'[19] He mentions Dawkins as a writer who has criticized Gaia on the grounds that it is contrary to the expectations of natural selection. This seems a somewhat dogmatic attitude, as though selfish genes have no right to co-operate to the extend of providing altruism on a global scale! Dr Lovelock has replied to such criticism by what he has called 'a parable of the daisy world', to show how natural selection can act as a sensor to regulate temperature near an optimal level for a specified life form.

Gribbin comments on Gaia in a way which suggests a similarity between the planet and the human person:

> It is however scarcely less likely that many different forms of life on Earth may be unconsciously maintaining the stability of the whole environment through a variety of checks and balances than that thousands of millions of individual cells, each of them a combination of earlier cell forms working in harmony, could co-operate to produce a human being, maintaining stability of bodily temperature, fighting off infection, and even providing self-awareness in an intelligent brain. Using language which would make a geneticist wince, we can even speculate that mankind was 'invented' by Gaia to serve as her own intelligent brain and nervous system, overseeing the whole planet and taking care of problems that cannot be solved so easily by unconscious feedback.[20]

When I wrote to Dr Lovelock to ask him how in his judgment Gaia came about and whether it could have preceded life, he responded in words which also suggest an analogy between Gaia and a biological organism:

> I have often speculated about it before your letter came. I speculated loosely that Gaia was a colligative property of life. Just as we are a colligative property of all our living cells. This could be, but if so it implies that life came first and Gaia was part of its development.

He went on to answer the particular question about which I had written to him:

> Your question raises the new speculation: could Gaia defined as a planetary tendency towards homeostasis [homeostasis refers to the ability of living things to remain in a constant condition in a changing environment] have preceded life? As you rightly surmise, if this is true, then our views about the

origins of life and in particular the randomness of its occurrence may need qualifying. For some time now it has been recognized that there is a tendency for numerous and varied ensembles to evolve towards homeostasis. Almost as if there were a fourth law of the universe as yet unformulated. Thus it might be that homeostasis is a property of ensembles in the universe in the way that gravity is a property of matter. So Gaia, if she exists, is inevitable.[21]

I raised that point in my letter because it seemed to me that the biosphere only produces the fine-tuning for a constant climate and for 3.4% salinity of the seas. There seems a prior tendency in inorganic nature to produce homeostasis, albeit in a somewhat rough and ready way. If it is true that, as Prigogine and his colleagues in Brussels have claimed, a steady state inorganic structure can, under the right conditions, change itself into a state which is more ordered than previously,[22] then it would seem no stranger that inorganic nature should have an inherent tendency towards homeostasis. I was interested therefore to receive a further letter later from Dr Lovelock when he kindly sent me an offprint containing the parable of the daisy world:

> The parable also sheds some new light on that lovely question you asked, 'which came first, life or Gaia?' It seems that a self-regulating homeostatic system is formed by taking no more than three fundamental properties of life, namely:
> 1. Exponential growth when food and environmental conditions are favourable.
> 2. The natural selection of those organisms which leave most progeny.
> 3. A set of physical constraints. This is, life can only flourish between certain ranges of temperature, moisture, solar radiation and abundance of a wider range of chemical species.
>
> It would seem likely that protolife, those chemical cycles that may have preceded life as such, was capable of performing in such a way as to meet the three conditions listed above. If so, then Gaia would have preceded life. Of course we shall never know for sure what happened all those aeons ago and it may not be all that important anyway.[23]

Whether or not Gaia preceded life, it remains only a *hypothesis*.[24] What is *fact* is that the constancy of climate and the continuing salinity of the seas have remained stable over vast periods of time. Whether the control mechanisms are purely inorganic or whether the biosphere contributes to these cybernetic systems remains a matter for debate. What cannot be denied is the remarkable stability of systems which are essential for the emergence of life in the oceans and for its consequent development.

We have to ask why these cybernetic systems exist at all. Are the laws of nature which govern these systems due to mere chance? Is the balance of oxygen in the atmosphere a merely random occurrence? Is there any particular reason why conditions on the planet have been optimal for life? Or does this just happen to be the case? Is the recycling of the trace elements which are vital for life one of those 'happy accidents' which makes it possible for life on Earth to evolve and develop? Is the present level of carbon dioxide in the air, in quantities sufficient to prevent a runaway greenhouse effect, another of those 'happy accidents' which makes possible the emergence of *homo sapiens*? Is it just luck that the salinity of the seas happens to stabilize itself at 3.4%?

These questions lead us to a further question. Do we have to extend the 'anthropic principle' from the field of cosmology into that of the biosphere? Using the weak form of the principle, are we to say that the human species is just very lucky to be alive? Or are we to use the stronger form of the principle, and assert that the existence of human beings as observers of the planet requires that these things should be so, and that we are as it were their cause? Do we have to imagine that, in an infinity of universes, there is bound to be one in which not only the constants of our physical universe obtain, but also a universe with a planet which has the particular tendencies towards homeostasis noted in this chapter?

It is entirely proper that scientists should continue to seek for scientific knowledge about the constancy of our climate over epochs of time, and about the stability of the saline proportions of sea water. Indeed there must be a scientific explanation of these phenomena which does full justice to all the facts. And whatever the scientific explanations may be, it will always be possible to hold that life on Earth is a purely random occurrence.

It seems to me, however, that another explanation becomes steadily more probable. As the number of 'coincidences' lengthens, and as their scope narrows from the universe to the planet, so it seems to me less and less probable that they are purely random. The laws under which they occur cry aloud for explanation. It seems to me more and more probable that these 'coincidences' are intended and contrived (in accordance with the laws of nature) so as to make possible the emergence of man.

5

The Emergence of Life

How did life begin?

A few years ago I was surprised to find myself reviewing for a scientific journal a book by Francis Crick called *Life Itself*. Crick, in conjunction with his colleague Watson, and building on the work of Rosalind Franklin, through his brilliant theory of the 'double helix', established the molecular basis of heredity. I had known Crick when we were both at Cambridge. I did not dare of course to comment in my review about the scientific contents of the book, but only on his disparaging remarks about religion; but even so he was able, perhaps not surprisingly, to write to me and put me right on the earliest fossil evidence for eukariotes (about which subject more later). I mention Crick's book here because in it he set himself the task of deciding whether it would have been possible for life to have been despatched to Earth from elsewhere in the universe by intelligent beings who wished to preserve it. (He judged that bacteria might possibly have been sent here by guided missile.) Others before him had suggested theories of 'panspermia', but not 'directed panspermia';[1] and in any case their ideas had been comparatively unsophisticated.

By contrast Fred Hoyle believes that life arrived here of its own accord from outer space, bacteria and viruses being embodied in comets and meteorites,[2] formed at the birthplace of new stars.[3] Hoyle does not believe so complex an organism as life could have evolved by chance on earth.

The probability of life appearing spontaneously on Earth is so small that it is very difficult to grasp without comparing it with something more familiar. Imagine a blind-folded man trying to solve the recently fashionable Rubik cube. Since he can't see the results, they must all be at random. He has no way of knowing whether he is getting nearer the solution . . . If our blind-folded subject were to make one random move every second, it would take him on average three hundred times the age of the Earth, 1,350 billion years, to solve the cube . . . These odds are roughly the same as you could give to the idea of just one of our body's proteins having evolved randomly, by chance. However, we use about 2,000 types of protein in our cells.[4]

Elsewhere Hoyle admits that not all the 2,000 enzymes required are independent of each other. 'But cutting down the numbers of enzymes from 2,000 does no good at all, unless the number were cut to a mere one or two, and this is not a viable suggestion.'[5] How then does Hoyle account for their existence? He believes that they must be explained by means of beings other than those known on earth:

Where did a knowledge of amino-acid chains of enzymes come from? To use a geological analogy, the knowledge came from the cosmological equivalent of a previous era, from a previously existing creature if you like, a creature that was not carbon-based, one that was permitted by an environment that existed long ago.[6]

This sounds reminiscent of *The Black Cloud*, a work of scientific fiction which Hoyle wrote many years ago! Hoyle's colleague and collaborator wrote to *The Times* to claim that 'the idea that life was put together by random shuffling of constituent molecules can be shown (in the words of Fred Hoyle) to be "as ridiculous and improbable as the proposition that a tornado blowing through a junk yard may assemble a Boeing 747"'.[7] This remark of Hoyle drew the President of the Royal Society to quote part of his anniversary address in response:

$10^{40,000}$ is an estimate of the chance that 2,000 enzymes molecules will be formed simultaneously from their component amino acids *on a single specified occasion*. The relevant thing however is the chance of some far simpler self-replicating system, capable of development by natural selection, being formed at any place on the Earth's surface, at any time within a period of the order of 10^8 years; the expectation of such events is wildly uncertain since we know neither the nature of the hypothetical self-replicating system nor the composition of the 'primaeval soup', but it is not obviously less than unity.[8]

We tend to think that natural selection should start with life. But considerable work has been done on the probability of prebiotic evolution. Schuster has produced 'a scheme for the logical sequence of steps in prebiotic evolution leading from unorganized macro-molecules to protocells'.[9] Eigen's researches into self-organizing cycles of macromolecules led him to assert that 'the evolution of life, if it is based on a derivable physical principle, must be considered an *inevitable* process despite its indeterminate course'.[10]

What are the requirements for life? Crick summarizes them thus:

The system must be able to replicate directly both its own instructions and indirectly any machinery needed to execute them. The replication of the genetic material must be fairly exact, but mutations – mistakes which can be faithfully copied – must occur at a rather low rate. A gene and its 'product' must be kept reasonably close together. The system will be an open one and must have a supply of raw material and, in some way or another, a supply of free energy.[11]

The emergence of life requires the natural evolution of a primitive cell, containing a membrane, DNA and enzymes. Could all these occur by chance? We do not know. Lightning and other reactions are likely to have formed organic molecules in the primitive 'chicken broth' of oceans. Nucleotides can assemble themselves into RNA. Nonetheless the difficulties are great. Orgel writes:

We do not yet understand in detail how the prebiotic soup on the primitive earth was formed . . . We must next explain how a prebiotic soup of organic molecules . . . evolved into a self-replicating organism . . . We do not yet understand even the general features of the origin of the genetic code.[12]

Crick writes with equal candour: 'An honest man, armed with all the knowledge available to us now, could only state that in some sense, the origin of life appears at the moment to be almost a miracle, so many are the conditions which would have had to be satisfied to get it going.' But he goes on to write:

> This should not be taken to imply that there are good reasons to believe that it could *not* have started on the earth by a perfectly reasonable sequence of fairly ordinary chemical reactions. The plain fact is that the time available was too long, the many micro-environments on the earth's surface too diverse, the various chemical possibilities too numerous and our own knowledge and imagination too feeble to allow us to be able to unravel exactly how it might or might not have happened such a long time ago, especially as we have no experimental evidence from that era to check our ideas against. Perhaps in the future we may know enough to make a considered guess, but at the present time we cannot decide whether the origin of life on earth was an extremely unlikely event or almost a certainty – or any possibility between these two extremes. [13]

Such frank statements about the origin of life are very striking. On the other hand, Crick's and Orgel's unspoken *assumption* is that life began by accident – that chance occurrences enabled a mechanism to assemble itself which was self-replicating and able to repair itself. This is an assumption that cannot be proved, any more than alternative assumptions can be proved – for example, that a vital factor entered into the first living system precisely when it came to life, or that new organismic properties emerged, so that under the influence of a morphogenetic field the elements assembled themselves into a living system. [14] Traditional science is violently opposed to the vitalism of the former, and somewhat muted about the organicism of the latter. Sheldrake puts succinctly the difficulties posed by an explanation of life that is totally mechanistic:

> The mechanistic theory postulates that all the phenomena of life, including human behaviour, can in principle be explained in terms of physics . . . This postulate is problematical for at least two fundamental reasons. First the mechanistic theory

could only be valid if the physical world were causally closed. In relation to human behaviour, this would only be the case if mental states had no reality at all or were in some sense identical to physical states of the body or ran parallel to them or were epiphenomena of them. But if on the other hand the mind were non-physical and yet causally efficacious, capable of *interacting* with the body, then human behaviour could not be fully explained in physical terms . . . From a scientific point of view the question remains open . . . Second, the attempt to account for mental activity in terms of physical science involves a seemingly inevitable circularity because science itself depends on mental activity. This problem has become apparent within modern physics in connection with the role of the observer in processes of physical measurement . . . Since physics presupposes the minds of observers, these minds and their properties cannot be explained in terms of physics.[15]

To bring the properties of *homo sapiens* into the argument when considering the obscure origins of life would seem to be putting the cart before the horse with a vengeance; but it provides a salutary warning at the outset not to accept the common assumptions of the natural sciences in considering what has happened in the dim and irretrievable past.

The basic element of all life of any kind is the cell. However it came into being, the cell is a chemical laboratory of immense complexity. Professor W. H. Thorpe writes:

The cell itself could not possibly function without the cell membranes which contain and selectively isolate the working parts of this laboratory. Biologists have long hoped to find a really 'primitive cell' illustrative of the stages between the supposed primitive acellular life and life as we know it now. But there seems little doubt today that there are no primitive cells living on the earth. All the cells that we know are of fantastic complexity. I believe that no biologist or physicist has yet been able to propose even the outlines of a theory as to how such a cell might have been 'evolved'. Monod himself sees that the evolution of even the simplest cell 'presents herculean problems'.[16]

There can be no life without a source of free energy which the cell (or before the cell fully evolved, the 'pregenote') could utilize. The primaeval bacterium, it is generally agreed, lived in an atmosphere which was without oxygen, and derived its energy from anaerobic fermentation. A great leap forward in evolution occurred when cells could use directly solar radiation as their energy source. Photosynthesis evolved, a process which is dependent on chlorophyll and through which carbohydrate is synthesized from water and carbon dioxide and from it (as by products) oxygen is released into the atmosphere. The structure of chlorophyll is somewhat complex, and its biosynthesis requires a number of different enzymes. Two distinct chemical systems are involved to produce this complex structure, which has been the foundation of most living creatures for three billion years. In one of these systems an enzyme is required to produce its components, and in the other another enzyme to put together the structure. (An enzyme is a complex molecule made of amino acids in a particular order to produce a three dimensional structure, and which acts as a catalyst by facilitating chemical reactions between particular substances.) One of the more remarkable results of photosynthesis has been to alter the Earth's atmosphere by the release of oxygen so that in due time the air was oxygen-based. Chlorophyll is green, and so produced blue green algae (an early form of bacteria). The fact that the natural world today is predominantly green shows the prevalence of chlorophyll systems some three billion years later. (An organism very similar to primaeval bacteria was recently found near Harlech in Wales, so that these early living beings have certainly persisted.) Scientists have theorized about how chlorophyll evolved and photosynthesis developed.[17] They may be able to explain how this mechanism evolved, but, as Gordon Rattray Taylor has written: 'Unless there was some inner necessity, some built-in primordial disposition to consolidate into such a pattern, it is past belief that anything so intricate and idiosyncratic should appear.'[18]

The next big evolutionary step forward was the evolution of eukariote cells, that is, cells which have a nucleus containing (among other things) the genetic material. In the original prokariote the genetic material was simply a ring of single-strand DNA in a bag. The eukariote is a much more sophisticated structure. Apart from the nucleus, the rest of the cell contains *mitochondria* which are full of enzymes and which have an apparatus which enables energy produced by oxidation to be used in the efficient combustion of the cell's energy. In addition it is able to ingest particles and has developed structures to digest them. It took two billion years for eukariotes to develop from prokariotes, and it is now thought that it happened through the process of 'endosymbiosis' by which one prokariote engulfed another, and both fused to produce a single living process. This may have happened several times, producing more and more complex cells. How did this come about? Was it mere chance? Was it due to some built-in primordial disposition? Was it even because of some extraneous influence? We do not know.

A further revolution took place which profoundly affected the whole future of evolution. Cells came together. For billions of years the Earth's oceans had contained various kinds of one-celled living organisms. Now, for reasons entirely unknown, they decided to join forces. We do not even know when this happened, but fossil record of such multi-celled organisms goes back 870 million years.

Some formed colonies, and these can still be seen today. For example, sponges are aggregates of cells which, even when minced up into individual cells, will join themselves together again. Slime moulds can behave in the most extraordinary ways. Normally this loose association of amoeba feed on bacteria and divide six or seven times a day. But suddenly some 40,000 of these amoeba come together to form a kind of slow-moving slug. This then lifts itself up vertically and forms a stalk, and a fruiting body develops at the head. When spores are released the whole edifice collapses and the amoeba die. What is the advantage of such behaviour over the more humdrum existence of the amoeba it is hard to see, and why such colonization developed is unknown.

A more important form of colonization is that of spinning spheres of photosynthesizing cells. The *volvox* is such an organism. Within this sphere some of its cells divide, and in time the original sphere breaks up and divided cells form new clusters. Meanwhile some of the individual cells may have decided to detach themselves from the colony and make a life of their own. Why did they originally congregate and form a sphere? Why did they detach themselves? We do not know. Of course the *volvox* is a contemporary organism, and we cannot be certain whether it existed in the early days of evolution. But the *volvox* has one characteristic which makes it of special interest for later evolutionary developments. It can turn itself inside out. One side becomes concave instead of convex, and makes a hole through the other side through which it pours itself, until the whole sphere is 'inside out'. If that process were to stop half way we would have the beginnings of the development of a more complex body – a tube with two ends, which in more mature organisms could develop into a gut with a mouth at one end and an anus at the other.

The most important association of cells were multi-celled organisms, metaphyta in the case of plants, and metazoa in the case of creatures. The cells associated to form a single organism. Once they had done this, the multi-celled organisms naturally enjoyed an advantage over the uni-cellular, and they predominated. Why did they associate in the first place? We do not know. The individual cells of the body learnt to specialize. Some formed themselves into muscle, bone and cartilage, some into skin, some into nerve tissue, and others perform various further specialisms. Some cells were biochemically very sophisticated. Some could perform many functions and secrete chemical substances, which others could not. The process by which this happens can be studied in research. But why did this process happen in the first place? We do not know.

As evolution 'took off' after the emergence of metazoan life, bodily shapes of the newly-emerged creatures developed. Head and tail formed in some cases, while others (such as jellyfish and starfish) adopted a radial symmetry. As bodies became more sophisticated, so more and more bodily organs were evolved, with greater and greater sophistication. How did internal organs develop? We do not know. It is often thought that this morphogenesis could be explained by what happens in embryonic development. However, this is not the case. Professor C. H. Waddington wrote: 'The embryonic stages of any highly evolved animal are never at all closely similar to the adult stages of its ancestors. They do however sometimes look like embryonic stages of the evolutionary ancestors.'[19] (The embryonic human being for example at one stage develops gill slits.) I was so puzzled about the way in which the internal organs of creatures have evolved that I wrote to a well-known authority on evolution who accepts the principle of natural selection. I was interested by the reply:

You asked for a source that would help you to understand how the viscera have evolved by natural selection. Perhaps I should point out that conventionally an explanation in those terms consists of little more than an argument that condition A is advantageous over, or better adapted than, condition B in given circumstances; natural selection is then assumed to have operated in transforming B to A. Soft structures, like the viscera, have no fossil record, and the only means of checking such explanation are embryonic development, which is assumed to reflect phylogenetic history, and comparative anatomy, through which the heart of a mammal, for example, may be interpreted by comparing it with those of crocodiles, frogs, lungfishes, lampreys, etc. Through studies of this sort one can convince oneself that the mammalian heart is suited to its task through modification of simpler or less elaborate structures. But natural selection, invoked as the explanation for the modification, would be employed as an axiom, not as a principle whose truth or universality was under examination.[20]

It became clear to me that, if the subsequent development of viscera could not be explained by natural selection, much less could their initial formation. How did creatures begin to form internal organs? We do not know.

There are many, many other questions concerning metozoa about which we would like to know the answers. How did sex begin? What force made bacteria inject into each other a portion of their DNA? If there is so much asexual reproduction in nature, and if the asexual usually predominates over the sexual when they both co-exist, what advantage is there in the latter? Perhaps there is a long-term advantage in flexibility through sexual exchange; but as Gordon Rattray Taylor puts it: 'How can selection favour a mechanism which will only show benefits in the future if at all?' A further key question concerns the ageing process. It is part of the law of life that cells die. Indeed the debris from dead organisms forms the food for new forms of life. Evolution could hardly have got under way if the earlier forms of life had lived for ever, for they would have prevented more complex forms of life coming into being. But how did the ageing process become written into living cells? Nobody knows. For me, however, the most difficult question posed by metozoa is put vividly by the late Gordon Rattray Taylor whose posthumous book on evolution I shall cite as shamelessly as I have in previous chapters quoted from Professor Davies and from Professor Lovelock, despite the adverse reviews it received in the Journal of the Institute of Biology. He writes:

> The trilobites were the first highly organized animals to populate the primordial seas, and they were everywhere. The first trilobite fossils came from the early Cambrian . . . The trilobites survived until the end of the Permian, a run of about 270 million years.
>
> They ranged in length from one-eighth to twenty-eight inches, but most were from three-quarters to three inches. The eye of arthropods, I must explain, is built on a totally different plan from the human or even the reptilian eye. It consists of closely packed columns each with its own lens at the top and photoreceptor at the bottom, the whole protected by a cornea. They are known as *ommatidia*. The columns are not quite parallel but are fanned out at the bottom . . . Specimens have been found with as many as 770 *ommatidia* in each eye . . . Each *ommatidium* produces its own image . . .
>
> The marvel of the trilobite eye became apparent only in 1973, when Kenneth Towe of the Smithsonian Institute reported that the lenses in the eyes of fossil trilobites consisted of precisely aligned crystals of calcite . . . They produced a sharp image at distances ranging from a few millimetres to infinity without further focusing . . . Calcite crystals emit light with the transparency of glass only if they are exactly aligned with the beam of light entering them . . .
>
> But that is only half the story . . . As far back as 1901 a Swedish worker had commented on the peculiar structure of the more evolved trilobite eyes. In 1968 Dr Clarkson began to investigate this structure . . . He found that the lens of these eyes was a doublet: an upper part of the calcite separated by a wavy boundary from a lower half of chitin.
>
> After Levi-Setti (of Chicago University) had delivered his lecture on the amazing light collecting properties of the trilobite eye, he had coffee with Clarkson, who told him of his work. Levi-Setti had a hunch that his doublet structure must

represent some form of optical correction ... One day, reading that bible of all students of vision, the *Traité de la Lumière* of Christian Huyghens, published in 1637, he found the description of an aplanatic or spherically corrected lens 'which resembled unmistakably the wavy shape seen in Clarkson's sketches'.

Huyghens' mention of some earlier results by Descartes led him to peruse the latter's *La Géométrie*, published in 1637. 'There I found a second construction somewhat different from that of Huyghens, but designed to perform the same function. This matched a second version of the trilobite lens shapes described by Clarkson.'[21]

I quote this extraordinary story at some length because it focuses so well some of the more difficult questions posed by the study of evolution. Dr Rattray Taylor comments on the story thus:

The trilobites evolved a lens shaped to correct for optical aberration identical to that proposed (quite independently of any knowledge of trilobites) by Descartes and Huyghens half a billion years later.

Why was such perfection needed? Dr Clarkson suggests that trilobites may have lived in very muddy turbid water. Or perhaps they only came out at night or at dusk ... To make the matter more puzzling, there is the fact that some trilobites were blind.

How did the earliest trilobites collect together the intricate genetic information needed to construct this semi-miraculous structure? And how strange that all that know-how should have been lost again when the phacopid line of trilobites became extinct at the end of the Devonian.[22]

Trilobites were only one group of species that emerged from the metozoan explosion of life. The sea was teeming with food in the form of uni-celled living organisms. It has been estimated that by the end of the pre-Cambrian age there was the largest variety of living organisms that the Earth has ever known – but of course they were all in the sea. Some of these forms still exist almost unchanged, like the oyster. It doesn't appear to have a very promising structure or shape, but it has lasted through millions of years until today. So too have cephalopods like the octopus or the squid. The gastropods tied themselves up almost literally in knots for reasons which are very obscure. Out of this wealth of marine life one form must have emerged from which eventually mammals evolved. No one can tell for certain which species this was.

From this very brief survey of life from its first emergence to the explosion of metazoa it has become apparent that because of the length of time that has elapsed, and because of our comparative ignorance of primaeval conditions and the scarcity (and ambiguity) of the fossil evidence, there are many questions which cannot be answered. If we are to look for a key which will unlock the mechanism by which life evolved, we shall have to look elsewhere than the earliest stages. There seems to be a built-in tendency towards greater complexity, but we cannot know whether this was an end in itself. Chance must have had a lot to do with the evolution of species and those most fitted to their environment would have survived to propagate themselves. That cannot be in doubt. The question, however, remains whether or not this is the *only* principle at work – chance mutations of genetic material producing changes which were perpetuated in those species most fitted to their environment to survive. If so, then evolution began as a blind process and leads up to man by random chance. As things stand, this process of natural selection seems to me improbable as sole cause. But that might be due to human ignorance about what actually happened. It remains an open possibility. Were there other forces at work as well? Is it more probable that, just as inorganic matter tends to organize itself in suitable conditions into more complex assemblies, so too living matter may have a similar tendency? If this is the case, then it is legitimate to ask why. Is it possible or even probable that there is divine influence at work on the whole evolutionary process? To attempt to answer this question, we must look at the later stages of evolutionary development.

There have been many stages. Over vast periods of time, life has emerged in multitudinous forms. It has been estimated that 99.9% of all species have become extinct: but there are still some two million different species alive today. (That means there must have been about two billion in all!) This gives some statistical indication of the number of living forms.

For our knowledge of these differing forms, in all their great variety, we are indebted to the fossil records. Fossil time is defined by the rock strata in which fossils are found. Nobody knows how long it was in advance of the fossil evidence that soft multi-celled animals in fact evolved. The *Cambrian* period began some 600 million years ago, and fossils of animals appear towards the end of the *pre-Cambrian*. The prokariote cells, as we have seen, produced blue-green algae and bacteria, some billion years ago. These evolved after a further billion years into one-celled eukariote organisms, amoebids and ciliates and minor protozoan groups. Out of this source there evolved eventually two of the three 'kingdoms' of living things, fungi and animals, both of which need organic material for their food. The third 'kingdom' of plants probably developed by a different route from the first prokariotes.

Here we must confine ourselves in the main to man's genealogical tree, although we cannot neglect the kingdom of plants because animals could never have emerged from the oceans on to the land unless plant life had developed sufficiently to sustain them.

By the end of the *Cambrian* (about half a billion years ago) there is in the fossil record evidence of abundant marine life, with the trilobites dominant. But this dominance was strangely followed by the extinction of two-thirds of all the trilobite families. During the *Ordovician* (500–425 million years) the first fishes appeared, but invertebrates were dominant. In the *Silurian* (425–405 million years) the first terrestrial plants and animals appeared. Then on land vegetation developed. During the *Carboniferous* (345–280 million years) numerous large-scale trees appeared, while sharks abounded in the oceans and amphibians on land. Towards the end of this period great coal forests and conifers grew on the land, and the first reptiles make their appearance in the fossil record. During the next period (*Permian* 280–230 million years) there was glaciation at low latitudes, and many marine animals (including the trilobites) became extinct.

After what is called the *Paleozoic* ('ancient life') there begins what scientists call the *Mesozoic* era ('middle life'). The first dinosaurs appeared during the *Triassic* (230–180 million years), and there were abundant conifers. During the *Jurassic* (180–135 million years) the first birds and the first mammals appear on the fossil records, with abundant ammonites in the oceans and still dinosaurs on land. The latter reached their climax followed strangely by their abrupt extinction, during the next age, the *Cretaceous* (135–163 million years), which also saw the advent of flowering plants.

There follows after the *Mesozoic* the *Cenozoic* era when mammals became dominant. Placental mammals first appeared in the *Paleocene* (63–58 million years), followed in the *Eocene* (58–36 million years) by many modern types of mammals. Large running mammals appeared by the *Oligocene* (36–25 million years) and the *Miocene* (25–13 million years) was marked by abundance of grazing animals. At the end of the Tertiary period, large carnivores made their appearance during the *Pliocene* epoch, which began about 13 million years ago. We have now come down to comparatively modern times! Early man appeared during the *Pleistocene* (between half a million and three million years ago), and 'modern man' did not evolve until a paltry 11,000 years ago, a very recent newcomer on the global scene. To attempt to condense a billion years of global history within the limits of a page or so is to invite well-deserved ridicule. This breathless scramble down the eras and epochs has been made in order to try to give some shape to the argument that follows about the reasons for this almost incredibly rich development of living forms.

Even today, with only 0.1% of all species still alive, there is a wonderful wealth of creatures. There are twenty-six living phyla of animals (and nine that have not survived). These phyla include some animals that have stayed the course for hundreds of millions of years. The mollusc and the horseshoe crab go back to the *Cambrian*, the shark to the *Devonian*. Even the humble cockroach can trace its ancestry to the *Carboniferous*, while the crocodile can boast a lineage reaching to the *Triassic*. Compared with these, man has hardly arrived.

The twenty-six surviving phyla range from sponges to chordates (vertebrates) within which fall mammals (all thirty-two orders of them). (Each kingdom is divided into phyla, and within phyla there are orders. There are further subdivisions into families, genera and species. There are of course intermediate forms, and there is some difference of opinion about what constitutes a species. The best description is that of the biologists – 'a group of populations that is inter-fertile'.)

The chordates include mammals, fish, reptiles and birds.[23] Examples from the twenty-five remaining phyla could include such varied forms of life as sea anemones, flat-worms, crabs, clams, sea squirts, and moss animals. (Different types of worm feature among the species of no less than thirteen different phyla.) Without illustrations it is not possible to give the tremendous variety of the forms and systems of living animals. Life has developed differently in differing environments. At first for example the Earth's atmosphere was very different from what it is now. Some areas were colder than others, some had particular types of flora, some were affected by particular ocean currents. In some areas there were glacial interludes; and the drifting continents, when they joined up, gave rise to altered habitats.

It is amazing to me that research enables us to know such a great deal of our predecessors. Knowledge about our global past has mushroomed over the last century. Is it possible to give a coherent account of the way in which this vast variety of life has developed? The question needs a two-fold answer. The genotype is the word used to denote the genetic constitution of a living animal which gives rise to its 'phenotype', which is its actual physical constitution and appearance, and which arises from the interaction of the genotype and its environment. If we are to return a coherent and full answer to the question posed by the evolutionary process, it is necessary to consider both how life developed from one species to another, and from one phylum to another phylum, and also to consider the genetic changes that made these constitutional alterations possible. To these difficult questions we must now turn.

6

The Evolution of Species

I have been greatly struck by the amount of emotion that is engendered both by opponents and proponents of the theory of natural selection. Perhaps it would be best, before entering this area of controversy, to be certain about what the theory of natural selection really is. I think that this is as good a description of it as any:

> The preferential survival and reproduction of those individuals born with a slight variation in character conferring some adaptive benefit or some advantage in coping with the demands of the environment. The variations were supposed to be produced by a purely random disturbance of the reproductive system, a process not understood in Darwin's time but subsequently identified with genetic mutation and recombination.[1]

This is very simple in essence, some would say deceptively simple. A slight difference occurs in a member of a species. The variation occurs because of some genetic change. If the variation assists the living organism, it will be reproduced in later generations. This will give an advantage to that individual and its progeny in the battle for life. Since there is only a limited amount of suitable food available and a limited amount of suitable space on earth, those individuals which inherit this added advantage will survive and breed more often, and others will tend not to survive. Thus changes that benefit an individual will tend to be selected and perpetuated. Most changes of this nature will be a disadvantage to a member of a species; such changes will therefore usually not be perpetuated, for a member of a species which exhibits such a change is likely to lose the battle for life, and will not reproduce. So slowly, gradually, a new species comes into existence through random mutation and natural selection of the fittest.

This is the theory. It has of course never been proved. In fact it could never be proved to be the sole mechanism of evolution without a disproof of all other possible mechanisms and without positive evidence of its operation. The theory is often known as Darwinism, but this is not quite accurate, because Darwin did not regard his theory as the sole explanation for the phenomenon of evolution. It is better known as neo-Darwinism, refounded on the basis of Mendel's theory of genetics and on the concepts of population dynamics developed by Sir Ronald Fisher and others.

Scientific theories are the product of the age in which they are conceived. They are usually in need of amplification and modification in the light of fresh intuitions. Thus Copernicus' view of the universe has been modified by Einstein's new insights. Euclidean geometry is modified by the new disciplines of topology. Quantum physics has modified mechanistic models of matter. And so one would expect scientists to regard Darwinism – or should I say neo-Darwinism – as a theory.

They don't, it seems, in the case of natural selection. Here many appear to have raised a theory to the status of a dogma, that is, a statement of belief that cannot be questioned without impiety. Rattray Taylor quotes, for example, Professor C. D. Darlington of Oxford, who said that to impugn Darwin's theory was 'ignorance and effrontery' and Professor Bernard David who wrote: 'Except for those sceptics who are willing to discard rationality, Darwin's theory has become Darwin's law.'[2] Lesser people often use more pejorative language.

When such emotion is aroused, it is appropriate to look for its cause. Professor Mary Hesse writes:

> It is quite clear that for the general public educated in Western society, scientific accounts of the origin and destiny of the world and of the status of human beings within it, have replaced the traditional mythical accounts given in various

forms in all religions, including in particular biblical religion. In other words, whatever other significance scientific theory has, it certainly has the status of cosmological myth in our society, as can be seen in the way 'origins' are taught in schools, and in the popularity of media presentations of fundamental science, both of physics and biology.[3]

If Professor Hesse is right, the story of how natural selection works in evolution forms one of the basic 'myths' which influence the imagination and affect the assumptions of the secular age in which we live. It therefore has a natural appeal to those nurtured on rationalism rather than religion. As William Temple wrote: 'It is obvious that for some students at least the impulse towards acceptance of "natural selection" as the one and only mode of evolution came from a mechanistic habit of mind and a desire at all costs to dispense with providential "design".'[4] Because the church has stubbornly upheld the established order, there was also a political aspect. As Hoyle has written: 'For centuries the doctrine of the special creation of species was seen as a moral justification for the Church's support for powerful autocrats throughout Europe. Not only were species held to be immutable, but men were thought to be fixed in their position in life by divine ordinance.'[5] There were particular reasons perhaps why 'natural selection' became immediately so popular in Victorian England when Darwin introduced it into public consciousness. Progress was an idea whose time had come. It is surely no accident, as Pelikan has pointed out, that Darwin wrote out a sketch for his great book *The Origin of Species by Means of Natural Selection* in 1844, the very same year in which John Henry Newman set down his general view which was later expressed in his book on development within the church.[6] As Barbour writes: 'What rescued the nineteenth century from the despair implicit in Darwinism? It was the fact that quite quickly in scientific minds blind Fate was transformed into a benevolent cosmic Progress.'[7] Moore points out how theologians took up this point, and quotes Drummond to the effect that, even at its 'very terrible price', evolution was 'none too dear' for the thing purchased was 'nothing less than the present progress of the world'.[8] Raven further points out that the theory was eminently congenial to be the broad characteristic of the contemporary outlook:

Life *was* a struggle: every businessman knew it and if he was honest admitted that a certain ruthlessness in securing the safe margin between success and failure was inevitable. Every little helped: thrift, utility value, the commercial significance of the trivial, this was the philosophy for a nation of shopkeepers. The weak to the wall: sentimentalism was all very well; 'Nature red in tooth and claw' was a nasty fact, but it was no use crying over it; a great nation could not afford to be squeamish; and if the survival of the fittest was a law of nature . . . ! So the arguments ran.[9]

Does such an account of the ready acceptance of Darwinism sound fantastic? Professor Hesse gives other examples of socio-logical reasons for the adoption of particular theories; for example, the acceptance of indeterminism in quantum theory in the Weimar Republic of Germany with its roots in romantic defeatism and the anarchism of post-war culture or the ready acceptance of an aether theory by Cambridge scientists of the last century who were sympathetic to psychic research and looking for an antidote to materialism.[10] Darwinism has been regarded as a bastion against Marxism, 'dismantling its theoretical basis'. And when, lately, there has been an attack on Darwinism in favour of 'evolution by jerks', such a theory of saltationalism has actually been attacked as Marxist, because it accords more with Communist theory. Nor can we forget how Lysenko, a third rate scientist, was promoted in the Soviet Union, precisely because he politicized the issues at stake in his opposition to neo-Darwinism and Mendelian genetics.

Lysenko's theories were disastrous in practice. They were not true. This raises the question of the truth of neo-Darwinism, even if it performs the function of an interpretative myth for a capitalist secular age. Is neo-Darwinism true or not? What are the criteria? Mary Hesse suggests that

> the forms of truth required for understanding both scientific theory and religious doctrine must be other than the 'objective truth' of instrumental science which is derived from its success in empirical prediction and control . . . In our account of the interaction of cognitive systems of different kinds, however, we need a quite different theory of truth which will be characterized by *consensus and coherence* rather than corre-

spondence, by *holism* of meanings rather than by atomism, by *metaphor* and *symbol* rather than literalism and univocity, by intrinsic judgments of *value* as well as of fact.[11]

The theory of natural selection cannot be proved by empirical prediction and control. We obviously cannot verify any predictions about future evolution. As Popper has written: 'Neither Darwin, nor any Darwinian, has so far given an actual explanation of the adaptive evolution of any single organism or any single organ. All that has been shown – and this is very much – is that such explanation might exist (that is to say they are not logically impossible).'[12] Only in matters of immunity do genes seem to mutate when a particular illness becomes, as we say, 'drug-resistant', or when insects become immune to toxics such as DDT. Despite thousands of fly-breeding experiments, no new species of fly has been produced. Selective breeding of wheat shows that it is possible to change a single wheat character, but not to bring about the kind of complex genetic change that produces altogether new phenotypes. It is often claimed that the change in colour of the peppered moth *Biston betularia* from grey to black as a result of an industrial environment is an example of Darwinism. It is certainly true that the black colour is now dominant where the grey used to be (although the Clean Air Act is tending to reverse this), whereas in a non-urban environment the black variety (which kept recurring) was easily seen by birds and therefore eaten. But this is not a *new species*. Moreover, 'more than seventy other varieties of moth were found to have darkened in industrial areas in Europe, the US and Canada . . . Why are the proportions surviving quite different in different species? Odder still, dark mutants appeared among ladybirds and spiders that are distasteful to birds whatever their colour.'[13] And why does another moth behave differently? *Phigalia titea* prefers a light background and in particular the light oak.[14] Darkened forms of moth exist and comprise 20% of the population. They would be expected either to seek a more appropriate background or to be exterminated.

In his autobiography *Unended Quest* Karl Popper wrote these words:

I have come to the conclusion that Darwinism is not a testable scientific theory, but a metaphysical research programme – a

possible framework for testable scientific theories. It suggests
the existence of a mechanism of adaptation and it allows us
even to study in detail the mechanism at work. And it is the
only theory so far which allows us to do that.

This is of course the reason why Darwinism has been almost
universally accepted. Its theory of adaptation was the first
nontheistic one that was convincing; and theism was worse
than an open admission of failure, for it created the impression
that an ultimate explanation had been reached.

Now to the degree that Darwinism creates the same
impression, it is not so very much better than the theistic view
of adaptation; it is therefore important to show that Darwinism is not a scientific theory but metaphysical. But its value
for science as a metaphysical research programme is very great,
especially if it is admitted that it may be criticized and
improved upon.[15]

And this, with the backing of such an eminent authority as Karl
Popper, is just what I hope to attempt.

The strength of neo-Darwinism lies in the conviction that there
is no known mechanism by which the genetic make-up of a living
being can be changed by its environment or its behaviour.
Medawar writes: 'In spite of very strenuous and not always very
scrupulous attempts to unseat it, nothing has yet occurred to
challenge the belief that the environment cannot act "instruc-
tively", i.e. cannot imprint specific information upon the genetic
system of living organisms.'[16] Since Medawar wrote those words
in 1977, an Australian biologist, Ted Steele, has attempted to do
just that.[17] In 1979 he wrote a book in which he suggested that
viruses could cause a mutation in a body cell which could spread
to other cells and finally the virus could spread this mutation to
the germ-cells of the organism. However Medawar with others
repeated these experiments and came to a contrary conclusion;
and the controversy is not yet settled. Steele may turn out to be
right or wrong. We cannot be sure. As Medawar had written
earlier: 'It would be foolhardy to say that we knew all that there
was to know on the subject, and that no new source of genetic
information will ever be discovered.'[18]

I must confess to a particular fellow feeling for Ted Steele, for I
understand that his doubts about the adequacy of the natural

selection hypothesis were crystallized after reading Arthur Koestler, and the writings of Arthur Koestler had the same effect on me.[19] It would of course be foolish and ignorant to denigrate in any way the theory of natural selection. It has stimulated an enormous amount of scientific research, and as Popper has said, its value as a metaphysical research programme is very great. The only question that arises here is whether it is the *sole* mechanism for evolution.

Neo-Darwinism certainly appears to have some grave difficulties to overcome if it is to give a coherent explanation of all the phenomena of evolution. One of the greatest difficulties concerns the comparatively short time span in which all the millions of mutations must have occurred and in which modifications to species and to phyla must have taken place. The whole span of evolution spreads over more than three billion years, but particular developments must have happened within comparatively short periods. For example, the first mammals did not appear until about 180 million years ago, and until the extinction of the dinosaurs they seem to have remained small and insignificant animals. From then onwards they appear to have proliferated; and between the first appearance of placental mammals sixty-three million years ago to the end of the Eocene about thirty-six million years ago, many modern types of mammal evolved. How did all this happen so comparatively rapidly? Furthermore, particular species seem to develop very rapidly also. For example, one island in Hawaii has 300 species of the fly *Drosophila* (but another island has only six). Some other species are notable for their proliferation, for which no good cause can be given. The Cichlids, for example, are fish which live in the great lakes of Africa, intelligent animals which communicate with each other by changes of body colour. They live in 'settlements' in the lakes and carry their young in their mouths. There are over 300 species. Orchids are a family with over 20,000 species.[20] Earlier in the process of evolution, there seems no explanation on Darwinian grounds for the large explosive radiations of life forms during the Mesozoic era. Nor is it easy to understand why some species have remained static for hundreds of millions of years, while others (such as *homo sapiens*) have evolved in the very recent past. It is no easier to explain why some genera have only one species, and some families contain only one genus.

A further difficulty lies in the inability of palaeontologists to produce sequences of organisms showing major evolutionary change. In the case of living organisms a comparison of their molecular structure is possible. But from fossils it is not possible to produce a neat genealogical tree showing how species, families, orders, classes emerged. There is a dearth of intermediate forms. We simply do not know the inter-relationships. It may be simply that the fossil record is very deficient because some forms of organism are more likely to fossilize than others. But I am surprised that it is not easier to trace out the lineage of past and present species.

One can mention puzzle after puzzle. Blood contains more than eighty components, including the vital haemoglobin which picks up oxygen from the lungs and releases unwanted carbon dioxide. Haemoglobin contains iron; but the ferric iron that is a trace element in food has to be changed into ferrous iron that can be stored in the liver. The stomach evolved hydrochloric acid which effects this change. Nobody knows how this evolution took place. Blood had a great advantage over sea water (which it seems to have replaced) because it can contain fifty times as much oxygen. Why are there four different human blood groups? It is well known that a person must have blood of the right group for a transfusion. Medawar writes: 'The raison d'être or survival value of differentiation into blood groups, that is the special function blood group differentiation fulfils, is not yet fully understood, and no one quite knows in what ways the subdivision of human beings into different blood groups is of any use.' Yet, on neo-Darwinian premises these different groups seem likely to have emerged and persisted because they convey an advantage; but perhaps they are 'neutral'. To take a very different example of perplexing evolution, it is hard to understand how a cow should have evolved such a very complex digestive system on neo-Darwinian premises. It is an efficient system, even if it requires a lengthy period of rumination; but a horse eats the same kind of diet as a cow, and its digestive system is far simpler. It is not easy to understand why the simple and complex system should persist side by side.

It is equally difficult to explain on these premises how multipurpose use came into being within the genotype. It is extraordinary that Ribonucleic Acid (RNA), which carries the genetic instructions and helps to assemble proteins for the vital processes of life, also serves as a means of governing some of the chemical reactions necessary for these processes.[21] I do not find it easy to comprehend, on the basis of neo-Darwinism, how this double use could have evolved. Similarly a double use has been detected in 'virtually every one of the hormones that control the unmentionable spasms and secretions of our digestive, reproductory and excretory organs'.[22] These also play a vital part in the more refined operations of the human brain. How did it come about that they could perform this double role?

A further difficulty may perhaps be added to the long list that has already been given. I refer to the strange phenomenon of mimicry. Professor Thorpe has commented that 'it powerfully suggests itself as evidence for a true though limited purpose'.[23] There is a great range of mimicry in nature, both visual and auditory. It is advantageous for a creature to imitate its predator, but it would seem to be much easier for a butterfly to adapt itself so that it shares the bitter taste of the species which it mimics rather than to imitate with such perfection the pattern of its bright colours. As for camouflage, this is not always easily explicable on neo-Darwinian premises. If polar bears are dominant in the Arctic, then there would seem to have been no need for them to evolve a white-coloured form of camouflage. A ptarmigan that turns white in the winter may be a variant of an albino strain, but the most improbable random mutations seem to have occurred for it to turn white only during the winter months and not during the summer as well, so that it can merge with its environment at all seasons.

One of the more interesting questions raised by the theory of natural selection concerns the evolution of altruistic behaviour in members of a species. It is easy to show that the 'selfish gene' can secure its survival in the population as a whole if 'one creature is willing to die for the species'. But it is not easy to show how altruistic behaviour is likely to evolve which will not be directly advantageous for other members of the species. For example, the warning cry of the jackdaw may save others from the predator, but it endangers an individual jackdaw betraying its location and presence. If behaviour evolves through the survival of the fittest, I do not find it easy to see how the theory can explain this warning cry.

Among the stranger problems remaining to be solved by the theory of natural selection is a matter which Professor Thorpe mentioned in 1961 and to which Sir Alister Hardy also drew attention in his Gifford Lectures in 1964 among his 'problems for current evolution theory':

> It concerns a little free-living fresh water flatworm called *Microstomum* which has only a very simple nervous system. It stores in the surface layers of its body the nematocysts or stinging capsules which have been produced by cells in the body of the polyp *Hydra* upon which it feeds in order to produce the weapons to use for its own defence. When *Microstomum* has sufficient nematocysts, it will no longer attach *Hydra* even though it is starving.[24]

The method by which the nematocysts are transferred from the gut to the surface of the body of the *Microstomum* are complex. Hardy quotes here Thorpe's own words:

> Here then is a specific drive or appetite satisfied only by a very indirect series of activities, the recognition and selection of a specific object, recognition of the undischarged stinging cells by the wandering tissue-cells, and some sort of 'perception' of its form so that it may be aimed. The uniform distribution of the nematocysts over the surface suggests a *gestalt*. So striking are these facts that Kepner was driven to postulate a group mind amongst the cells of the body to account for the internal behaviour of the *Microstomum*. Such a conclusion seems to us absurd; but it is to be remembered that behaviour such as this, while striking the ethologist as amazing, is a commonplace of embryology – though the embryologist has no better theory for explaining it than the ethologist.[25]

Hardy comments: 'There is indeed point in what Thorpe says.'

Some phenomena powerfully suggest that characters acquired by an individual during its lifetime somehow find entry into the genome, and become inherited from generation to generation. Lamarckism is the name usually given to this hypothesis, although it formed only one part of J. B. Lamarck's original theory. Waddington's theory of 'genetic assimilation' demonstrates how natural selection from the gene pool can produce a simulated Lamarckian effect. But can it really explain how the unborn chick of an ostrich has calluses on its rump, pubis and breast (which will be in contact with the ground on an adult ostrich)? I find it hard to understand how natural selection from a gene pool (which contained some random mutations) gave rise to this, and at the same time proved advantageous for survival. A further example is the human hand. A baby is born with prefabricated flexure lines on its hand; and what can be the survival value of these? Lamarckians claim that their theory accounts for the withering away of an organ after disuse, but the shrinking of a whale's thigh bone to a mere eighteen inches after its return to the oceans seems hard to account for on either neo-Darwinian or Lamarckian premises. Some experiments have been claimed as favourable to Lamarckism, such as inducing changes in flax by the use of fertilizers. The theory lost credibility in this century when Kammerer was accused of faking evidence about the nuptial pads of the midwife toad. It has never been a popular theory in this country, although interest in it has been recently aroused by Ted Steele's hypothesis concerning viruses about which mention has already been made.

Lamarck claimed that the behaviour of an animal, if it altered, would lead to an alteration of its physical constitution. Changed behaviour would produce changed needs and these would produce adaptation in the creature which could be inherited.[26] Since Lamarck's day ethologists have studied in detail the behaviour of animals. Alteration in behaviour can indeed sometimes be shown to precede structural change; but this in itself does not invalidate the neo-Darwinian hypothesis. It could be that changes of, say, feeding habits come first, and these changes are assisted by random mutations which are perpetuated in those members of a species which are benefited by them. Professor Sir Alister Hardy, who is himself a neo-Darwinist, has given a new twist to neo-Darwinism by suggesting that behaviour is itself a selective force.[27]

Animal behaviour is a complex subject; and Rattray Taylor is helpful in pointing out different kinds of such behaviour. Some is automatic (as when two birds take it in turns to sit on a clutch of eggs, and one departs even though the other has not arrived to take over). Some behaviour seems pointless, as when an eight-legged spider mimics a six-legged ant. Some behaviour is easily intelligible, as for example that of a coconut-eating crab (without too much brain) which seems to know by instinct that there is milk inside the coconut. There are countless instances of animal behaviour which it does not seem feasible to explain as the result of precise genetic instructions, and I cannot see how such behaviour came into existence on neo-Darwinian premises. Such behaviour can seem intelligent, even purposive, and insightful. It can seem to manifest curiosity. Why do sweat glands increase in number in the tropics? Why does skin harden from use? By genetic assimilation? Lamarckism is an attractive proposition even if there is no mechanism which can be demonstrated to operate it. But Lamarckism would not solve all outstanding problems. Why do chicks peck at the one place in the egg where there is an airspace? Is this behaviour really imprinted in their genes? How do species of beetles build a complex kind of nest after emerging from three years in the wood, without any opportunity for learning such behaviour? Is this too imprinted with precise instructions in their genes? As I was writing this section, I came across a further puzzle concerning the bonding of lambs and ewes to which I could see no easy explanation.[28] This bonding must begin immediately after birth if the lamb is to survive. The ewe must respond to the newborn lamb, they must keep together and the lamb must feed within the first hour or so. How does the bonding take place? It seems that the lamb responds to the mother's waxy secretions in its inguinal pouch near the base of its udder, having grown to recognize these from the womb. The ewe in turn responds to the lamb by detecting the smell of its own amniotic fluid, which stimulates the ewe to approach and lick the newborn lamb. If lambs were to survive, some form of bonding must have evolved right from the beginning of their evolution. Was it just good fortune that there happened to be these two means of recognition? They could hardly have evolved through 'the survival of the fittest' because without them it is unlikely there would have been any survivors at all! This is only one example of many similar matters of animal behaviour which have evolved. It would be helpful if those who believe in neo-Darwinism could provide us with a few more scenarios to show how a series of small random mutations would be likely to bring about the evolutionary changes that have in fact taken place. The mammalian reproductive cycle has always struck me as particularly difficult to explain on these principles; and especially the birth process. Before the days of caesarean section and substitute milk, no human baby would have been born alive and subsequently survived without a three stage labour on the part of its mother, the full dilation of her cervix, and the stimulation of her mammary glands to produce first colostrum and then mother's milk. What triggers off this syndrome and how did it evolve? I don't suppose we can ever know.

Whether or not there is any truth in the Lamarckian hypothesis, neo-Darwinism seems inadequate to explain many of the complexities of animal behaviour. Raven cites the case of the parasitism of the common cuckoo as an instance of co-ordinated behaviour for which the theory of natural selection seems sadly inadequate. He describes how the eggs of a cuckoo have to be laid before those of the birds it will supplant, how it is fed by its foster mother, and how it ejects its step-brothers and sisters from the nest.

> It will be seen that each one of this sequence of conditions is essential for the success of the whole. Yet each by itself is useless. The whole *opus perfectum* must have been achieved simultaneously. The odds against the random occurrence of such a series of coincidences are, as we have already stated, astronomical. Nor could a single accidental performance if it should happen establish any guarantee of its fixation and repetition.[29]

Another type of remarkable behaviour is seen in migrant birds. They can find their way precisely from one place to another thousands of miles away; and they can return (as swallows do) to precisely the same nest from which they left. No doubt there is a variety of means by which they do this, with an inbuilt magnetic and celestial compass, to say nothing of learnt skills.[30] The mechanism is imperfectly understood, but it is not easy to comprehend how such behaviour could have evolved solely through natural selection. Similarly why do eels go to the Sargasso Sea and why do salmon, after travelling for thousands of miles, return to the same point of the same river from which they first emerged as parr? Once again it is easier to ask these questions than to answer them.

One of the stranger types of animal behaviour is seen among

termites. Termites dispose of most of the dead vegetation of the tropics and without them the world would be a very different place. The Macrotermitinae of West Africa use their faeces to break down the fungi which they cultivate in the combs which they build from their faeces. This enriches it nutritionally and the termites subsequently reconsume the fungus-faeces mixture, thus utilizing virtually 100% of their food.[31] I was greatly intrigued by Professor Morrison's annual Bronowski Lecture on termites in 1979. He was describing an African species of termites which lives off fungus which they sow, crop and eat inside warm deep chambers of their nest (which may contain up to a quarter of a million individual termites). The nest is crowned by a perfect arch made by the insects:

> To begin with there are simply the scurrying insects in the dark, each one individually making a little pile of pellets . . . At some moment each apparently comes to obey an internal programmatic rule, which in effect says . . . 'Abandon your pile if and only if there is within your purview . . . a large pile. If there is, drop your work and go to work on the large pile . . . ' A third important signal arises in the system. This says: If you have a column at a certain height, and there is no column nearby of an adequate height, abandon the column you are working on and join one which by chance belongs to a pair. The fourth instruction says: When a pair stand close enough, a few among many columns as chosen by random events, close enough so that they might be practically bridged together, work at the tops until you bridge them across with cemented wood fibres to make the true arch.[32]

I was so fascinated by this description that I wrote to ask Professor Morrison how such behaviour could have arisen by natural selection. He responded guardedly: 'I think that it is fair to say that we do not yet understand the entire chain behind any but the simplest behaviours.'[33]

Creatures seem to have been born with varying degrees of instinct, insight, initiative, curiosity, and they display at times patterns of very complex behaviour. There are those who hold, with the socio-biologists, that all these are programmed in their genes, together with other programmes for the maintenance of their living systems. Not everyone, however, believes in the existence of all these genetic programmes, and some who hold that these programmes do exist do not believe that they are all the result of natural selection.

The genetic material of which Crick and Watson discovered the coding mechanism contains four different chemical units (nucleotides) repeated in an apparently random linear sequence millions of times over. This giant molecule is densely packed within a very small space in the cell. For example, the DNA of a bacterium contains some three million nucleotides which provide the codes for about 3,000 genes. It is reckoned that the genetic material for a human being contains some three billion nucleotides (or coding units) and between 30,000 and 150,000 genes – nobody knows how many. Errors in this huge chain of three billion units are rare, but when they occur they form the mutations which are the stuff of the evolutionary process.

The nucleotides are read off in groups of three to translate the DNA sequence into the linear sequence of amino acids that make up the proteins in a cell. These proteins may have a structural function or act as enzymes to carry out the many functions that occur in cells. A single error in one group of three can mean that the coding instructions are entirely changed, because the new triplet may result in the insertion of a different amino acid and this may change the structure or annihilate the function of the protein concerned. Thus a small mutation can have an enormous effect. However, it is known that many such errors can be tolerated or corrected to protect the organism from these harmful mutations.

It was discovered that a gene could be composed of a sequence of coding regions interspersed with non-coding regions ('nonsense DNA') which had no part to play in specifying the amino acid sequence of the protein concerned. These 'nonsense' sections are known as 'introns' and the protein-coding regions as 'exons'. Split genes of this kind are found in most higher organisms including man. They provide a means of generating new genes by stitching together exons from different old genes to generate new proteins with modified functions. Furthermore by stitching these exons together in slightly different ways great diversity can be generated in a single class of proteins. This appears to be the case for the antibody molecules which we need for protection against harmful agents.

Genes also seem to be able to jump from one position in the DNA and insert themselves elsewhere. Transposition of genes can occur within an individual cell type but there are also mechanisms to transfer genes from one organism to another. This is seen for example in the transmission of antibiotic resistance. Special elements of DNA exist called 'transposons', which transfer rogue genes very readily and rapidly. Viruses can act in the same way, carrying genes from one infected bacterium to another. Such genetic transfer mechanisms can lead to the build up of redundant DNA or multiple copies of certain genes. In some situations this multiplicity of gene copies is useful to produce large amounts of the relevant gene product at certain times in the cell's life and there appear to be mechanisms which evolution has developed to enhance this process. Very little is known, however, about the function of much of this apparently redundant DNA. The effect of all these discoveries is to suggest that the genome is far less stable than it was thought to be; but nobody knows how these mechanisms are controlled, or what is their real function. It could be, however, that they will be able to explain phenomena which at the moment seem somewhat baffling.

For example, changes should be gradual, according to the neo-Darwinian hypothesis. Over the centuries mutations will gradually accumulate so that slowly species change their structures. But this does not always seem to have been the case. There have been apparently sudden changes. There was an explosive radiation in the Mesozoic. Later there was profusion of the reptile family and later still, a further profusion of mammals. Speedy co-ordinated development seems to have taken place. There have long been theories of saltations, which have recently been revived. Stephen Gould has written of legitimate forms of macro-mutation which 'include the rapid saltatory origin of a key feature (around which subsequent saltations may be moulded) and large outward changes caused by small genetic changes that affect rates of development in early ontogeny with cascading effects thereafter'.[34]

Whether or not Gould's ideas will eventually find favour is uncertain, but there are certainly matters to be explained. As one form has given way to another, a fin evolves into a leg, scales evolve into feathers, legs evolve into wings. Massive structural changes are required to enable vertebrate life to migrate from the sea to the land; and these changes needed to be co-ordinated. When reptiles came to land, the fertilization of eggs in water by the male had to give way to another method. Nobody knows how the reptilian egg evolved. It is a beautifully complex organ with an amniotic sac and another sac for waste products secreted by the growing embryo. How and when did this evolve? Were amphibians originally viviparous? Nobody knows. Here indeed was a saltation.

The reptiles diversified into a number of groups, such as dinosaurs, and flying reptiles and snakes. We do not know how this diversification happened so quickly. The emergence of birds poses some equally awkward questions. Feathers are said to have evolved from the scales of reptiles, but if this occurred there is no evidence of intermediate structures. (Feathers for flying are different from those which conserve heat.) The modification requirements for a reptile to fly were considerable, and include reduction of weight, the alteration of its centre of gravity, and the strengthening of its pelvis, together with the modification of its brain to handle problems of balance and co-ordination. The metabolism required to be changed in order to produce enough energy for flight. Somehow all this co-ordinated development took place within the 200 million years which elapsed between the first emergence of vertebrate life from the oceans and the appearance of the first specimen of Archaeopteryx.

Great changes too were needed for the transition of reptile to mammal. In only fifty million years some twelve different groups of mammals appear in the fossil record from very different environments. Mammals bear their young alive, and they have a four-chambered heart, an insulating cover of hair and a more or less constant body temperature. They seem to have developed either as marsupials and placentals, but the placentals caused the virtual extinction of marsupials except in the isolated continents (as they had by then become) of Australia and South America.

These changes did not affect the kingdom of animals alone. Similar changes appear in the kingdom of plants. For example the angiosperms (flowering plants) appear as it were from nowhere. (The angiosperms protect the ovules in the carpel, but the gymnosperms such as conifers have no such protection.) Angiosperms suddenly appear in the fossil record, no one knows how.

(Co-ordinated change is not confined to phyla. It can apply equally to the development of species, and it can be equally perplexing. Rattray Taylor cites the case of the python's jaw. It is hinged, with two carved fangs which hold the victim while the python begins to swallow it. The angle of the teeth points backwards, so that they are of use only to a hinged jaw. However did this co-ordinated development occur?)

Gould has suggested that a species selection rate rather than a natural selection rate of individuals may give a causal explanation to saltations. Maybe the new genetic discoveries can shed some light upon it. Once a particular path is taken in evolution other changes naturally follow; it is however by no means clear that they are caused solely by natural selection. Some other force seems to be at work.

There are some other aspects of the evolutionary process which seem to support such a viewpoint.

1. Extreme perfection

It is not easy to understand how natural selection could bring about the number of instances of 'extreme perfection' (the phrase is Darwin's). Raven cites as an example of an *opus perfectum* the design and construction of its web by a common Diadem Spider. He describes how his friend Dr Bennett responded to this design. He told him:

> It is impossible for one who has watched the work for many hours to have any doubt that neither the present spiders of this species nor their ancestors were ever the architects of the web or that it could conceivably have been produced step by step through random variation; it would be as absurd to suppose that the intricate and exact proportions of the Parthenon were produced by piling together bits of marble.[35]

The most obvious example of 'extreme perfection' is the eye, which has evolved so many times in the history of evolution but each time on a somewhat different plan. I have already discussed earlier the extraordinary development of the trilobite eye hundreds of millions of years ago. The 'reinvention' of the eye seems to me no less remarkable. The fact that it has evolved at least three times suggests that it has a high probability rating. I suppose we must assume that selection from similar random mutations occurred in different species. The eye is specially important because it enables a predator to see its prey, but on neo-Darwinist principles the importance of an organ does not guarantee its appearance, nor does it account for its re-appearance. In 1980 I had recently read Archdeacon Paley[36] on the human eye as evidence of design, and I happened to notice that Sir Alan Hodgkir. was lecturing on the eye at the Royal Institution, and I wrote to him to ask him how it had developed. He replied:

It is difficult for scientists to say how the human eye evolved because there are few clues from the fossil record. This is true for most soft tissues. One of the striking things about 'eyes' is their astonishing diversity, ranging from simple eyespots to visual pits or pinhole cameras as well as compound eyes (present in the Trilobites 600 million years ago) and eyes with proper lenses which are found in cephalopods and vertebrates. Animals which zoologists regard as closely related to very ancient creatures tend to have simple eyes. For example the pearly Nautilus has a pinhole camera type of eye whereas squids and cuttlefish have lenses; the lancelot Amphioxus has eyespots whereas most other chordates have eyes with lenses.

One can guess how certain structures developed but most scientists are reluctant to air guesses in the popular scientific press and I can't give you any satisfactory references. There is a good but heavy book called *The Vertebrate Eye and its Adaptive Radiations* by G. L. Walls published by Hafner. There are a few references in David Attenborough's *Life on Earth* and a number of specialized handbooks on Sensory Physiology or Comparative Physiology which would give you some idea of the great diversity of visual receptors.

The difficulty in understanding how complex organs evolved is not new. One of the classical examples (raised by Romanes) is that of the electric fish. Here one asks how an elaborate organ generating several hundred volts could possibly have evolved by mutation and natural selection when we know that a simpler organ generating say a volt would be no use in electrocuting prey. This problem has become easier since my friend Lissmann discovered weak electric fish which have small electric organs that they use to detect objects in muddy water. Discoveries of this kind help one to understand evolution but I doubt whether we shall ever know exactly how the human eye evolved. Nevertheless it doesn't seem unreasonable, on the basis of a wide range of observations, to say that the human eye could have evolved by natural selection of random mutations.

I am not an expert on evolution, but I hope these somewhat random remarks may be helpful.[37]

I was grateful for this careful and courteous reply, but the problem still remains, at least concerning the human eye. How could an organ so complex evolve? Even more extraordinary than the evolution of the eye is the evolution of the ear. It seems to have developed from the lateral line of fish. This would have involved adapting an organ of vibration reception so that it became also an organ of hearing, and resulted in a very considerable modification of intricate bone structure and other complex changes and adaptations, including the grading of sensory hairs according to length, and a convenient deposit of crystal in the one place where it will register gravity. All by selection of programmes differing in mutations?

2. Overshoot

In some species tendencies seem to have gone too far, certainly further than are easily explicable on the grounds of natural selection. A favourite example of this is the case of the Irish elk. Its horns weigh nearly a quarter of a ton. Even if large horns are useful in sexual combat, there comes a time when, as with Goliath, a vast armoury is a disadvantage; even a disadvantage to both combatants, if the horns interlock.[38] A further example of overshoot is the mastoden. Its horns were so curved that they could only act as a buffer, and would have been useless for attack. The lyre bird has evolved an enormously long tail which must handicap its walking as well as its flight.

The most famous example of all is the peacock. 'The shimmering psychedelic display is a familiar symbol of natural glamour. Over one hundred feathers, some more than 120cm in length, and each adorned with a blue and bronze irridescent "eye" are raised and spread in an enormous fan which dwarfs the body of its owner. The tail of the peacock is as eloquent of the aesthetic senses of animals as was the song of John Keats' nightingale. But what exactly is it for, and how did it come to have such an elaborate pattern?'[39] How indeed? Hardy comments on the peacock:

> I have little doubt that the 'design' is coded in the DNA, as is the structure of the feathers and the instinctive reaction of the females to the design; yet with the great variability of the gene complex which we have previously discussed, I remain puzzled that the design, the *plan* of its layout, is indeed so constant.[40]

But why was it necessary to evolve this gorgeous design (and for it to remain constant) in order to stimulate the female to co-operate in the sexual act? Why did natural selection necessitate such perfection? I have not found an answer to this question.

3. Larval change

Remarkable changes take place in those organisms which metamorphose from a larval state. Every child who lives in the country knows how a tadpole changes into a frog. The differences between the two are not merely morphological. 'The haemoglobin of a frog is different from that of a tadpole. Different digestive enzymes are required,' wrote Rattray Taylor. 'In the metamorphosis of insects the change is even more striking. A larva is singularly unlike a butterfly both in appearance and in mode of life. The structural changes are far reaching, involving nerves, muscles, gut, sense organs, respiratory system, circulation, fat bodies, skins, alimentary canal, etc.'[41] He goes on to tell the story of the red eft, a variety of newt, which after three years on land, metamorphoses back again to a water born newt, losing its tongue and regaining its lateral line. These phenomena suggest that one set of genes in the genome may have been switched off and another switched on.

Koestler has pointed out the way in which in certain circumstances evolution may as it were retrace its steps along a pathway which led to a dead end, and make a fresh start in a more promising direction. 'The crucial point here is the appearance of some useful evolutionary novelty in the *larval or embryonic* stage of the ancestor, a novelty which may disappear before the ancestor reaches the adult stage but which reappears and is preserved in the *adult stage of the descendent*.'[42] Koestler gives as an example of paedomorphosis the larvae of a primitive organism like a sea urchin or a sea cucumber. These larvae unlike the adults have a bilateral symmetry like a fish with a ciliary band. Perhaps these larvae gradually became more fishlike, and reproduced themselves, and evolved into species more 'advanced' than adults of their original species. Perhaps from these there evolved in time chordates, and then vertebrates, and then mammals, and even finally *homo sapiens*. They may be the remote forebears of the human race! This is pure speculation (but none the worse for that); but if it happened it suggests some regulatory control – we know not what – of the genetic material which was responsible for the larval form.

4. *Development of embryos*

We have already noted Professor W. H. Thorpe's remark that the embryologist is no better than the ethologist at explaining the programmatic movement of cells within an internal organism. The embryonic cells sort themselves out under some kind of instructions. Cells of a young vertebrate embryo have been found to reassemble themselves if dissociated. These experiments have been carried out with liver, kidney and heart cells. When mixed together these cells can sort themselves out. In a normally developing embryo cells form themselves into the most complex shapes as a result of instructions, moving from one part of the embryo to another. An appropriate part of the embryo 'knows' how to grow into a leg, say, rather than a foot.[43] It has been suggested that bioelectricity plays some part in this process.[44] The details of the process are largely unknown. Professor Waddington wrote:

> How are all the activities of all the genes concerned in any developmental pathway tied together, so that they proceed in an integrated and orderly manner?. . . It seems certain that these answers, whatever they turn out to be, will have to centre around the nature of the substances that go to, and modify the activity of, the genes – the genotropic substances.[45]

There is control mechanism at work about which little at present is known, although several theories exist.

There is a further puzzle here. Professor Hardy has drawn attention to the strange phenomena of transformations in shape and size originally pointed out by D'Arcy Thompson. If an animal outline is superimposed on a drawing of horizontal and vertical co-ordinates with latticed squares, then others belonging to the same zoological group will often fit within a similar pattern at similar points, providing that the drawing is redrawn with certain simple mathematical distortions.[46] Medawar has taken up the suggestion that there is a similar type of transformation which occurs in human development, as between, say a foetus of five months and an adult. It is not easy to see how such a mathematical structure of growth could have evolved, at least on neo-Darwinian premises.

5. Repetition

Many features of different organisms have repeated themselves at different times. Bioluminscence has arisen many times in different species. We have already noted the evolution of the eye and ear on more occasions than one. Marsupials and placentals have at times evolved in parallel ways. Parallel development has also been noted in the kingdom of plants. It is not easy to suppose that the same random mutations have occurred in these different kinds of creatures. It is rather easier to suppose that similar forces are at work in the evolution of each. No doubt certain characteristics would appear in more than one line of evolution because the organism, having as it were 'chosen' to go down one path rather than another, develops in one way rather than another with consequent changes to its structure. Parallel development, however, suggests more than similar constraints; that there is some overall plan or purpose.

The possibility of this overall plan or purpose is suggested by many more characteristics than parallel development. The existence of trends over millions of years as well as repeated occurrence of the same evolutionary process, particular adaptations and changes which call for co-ordinated modifications – these and other tendencies seem to suggest some kind of overall plan behind evolution. Some of the stranger phenomena like 'overshoot' suggest that a tendency once started in the genome has not been able to be switched off, so that it develops beyond the point of utility.

If there is an overall plan, then it is by no means clear. There are so many cul de sacs, dead ends, false starts, and so much apparent meaninglessness in the records of evolution. And yet the hypothesis of natural selection seems inadequate to cover all the phenomena. How *could* these strange processes all have occurred by natural selection? Inevitably chance has played a very large part in the story, and natural selection is inevitable; but is this the *whole* story?

It is not impossible that the theorists of the neo-Darwinist hypothesis may be able to give a coherent explanation on their premises of all the strange phenomena that have been mentioned here. (Inevitably there has been concentration on those aspects of evolution which seem difficult to explain by way of natural selection, and those that are more easily explicable have largely been passed over.) Natural selection certainly remains a *possible* explanation of the whole field of evolution. No clear picture seems to emerge. Behaviour has some effect on adaptation, but no mechanism for the inheritance of acquired characteristics has yet been discovered which can account for changes between species. (Genetic assimilation is not the same as inheritance of acquired characteristics.) Once a species has begun to adapt in one direction certain other changes seem to follow naturally, and there is no going forward in some other direction (although there is always the possibility of standing still). The genome seems to have some hidden mechanisms for switching genes on and off, so that forms change. But it is difficult to see how 'jumping genes', 'transposons', 'introns' etc. can account for all the unexpected twists of evolution.

It seems to me less probable that natural selection can account for the whole evolutionary process than that other forces are also at work. There seems to me some process at work, similar to what we have already noted in inanimate nature as well as in the most primitive forms of life, whereby matter tends to assemble itself in more complex forms of living forms, not in a straightforward line to *homo sapiens*, but in a way that makes it probable that sooner or later *homo sapiens* will evolve.

It was encouraging for me to discover that there is a considerable number of eminent scientists who do not think that neo-Darwinism can account for all the evidence of evolution. I realize that the strength of the hypothesis lies in the fact that there is no known way by which information can enter the genome to alter its genetic instructions in a predetermined direction and there is no known way other than through the genome through which instinctive patterns of behaviour or physical structure can pass from generation to generation, or change over many generations. Therein lies the great strength of the hypothesis. At the same time the problems that it faces in trying to account for some of the difficulties seem to me if not insuperable, at least improbable.

I must admit that I felt a great sense of relief when I reached this conclusion after attempting to study the literature. I had long *felt* that the hypothesis could not cover the many complexities of behaviour and of morphological change, but feeling is different from understanding. There are of course those who believe that neo-Darwinism is compatible with the assumptions of the Christian faith:

> If we proposed that the world owes its being to a Creator God then I see no reason why God should not allow the potentialities of his universe to be developed in all their ramifications through the operation of random events; indeed, in principle, this is the only way in which all potentialities might eventually given enough time and space, be actualized.[47]

Habgood insists that neo-Darwinism is the mechanism of divine creativity:

> Random mutation in the genetic material throwing up new possibilities for biological existence, appropriate combinations selected out, first of all in the process of embryonic development, and then if successful tested in the actual business of living through many generations – this is the combination of chance and selection which drives the engine of biological creativity. Perhaps in other aspects of the universe as well, it is the element of chance which makes new developments possible. 'Time and chance governs all . . .' Is this a godless vision? I do not believe so.[48]

This is certainly not a *godless* vision, but it is one that is hard to reconcile with the God who is the Father of our Lord Jesus Christ. This kind of God winds the clock up and lets it run down, confident that through trial and error and blind chance what he wants will in the end turn up. He is the God of the deists, remote, unmoved, unloving. Chance and necessity may produce creativity, but they cannot produce purpose. And whatever else we may hope to say about the nature of God, we would surely wish to say that his creation of the world is purposeful rather than merely experimental; and that he is not remote from its processes. We do not want a God who is 'proprietor of a casino'.[49]

However unwelcome neo-Darwinism may be, it is a scientific hypothesis to be considered on the merits of the evidence. There is no evidence at all to support the thesis of the Creationists that God created the world in seven days, and that the biblical narrative of Genesis is an accurate scientific account of what really happened. Because no one particular theory can be proved to be the sole explanation of evolution, this does not mean that the whole of evolution is mockery. For all their concern for the 'Rock of Ages' rather than the ages of rocks, the Creationists do justice to neither. I cannot emphasize strongly enough that I am not in any way questioning the fact of evolution, but only its interpretation. Evolution itself is not in doubt.

In previous chapters I have argued that it seems probable that the universe has not developed solely by chance. That degree of probability is increased by a study of evolution. As we look at the big bang, the development of the cosmos or the formation of the atmosphere and the ecology of the planet, the probability of some other explanation than chance seems increasingly appropriate. Consideration of the actual phenomena of the world has been necessary, lest the impression were given that conclusions had been reached away from the evidence.

If God initiated the whole process of existence from the big bang onwards – and so far this seems to me the more probable explanation of all the complex phenomena of existence – then why did he not create life on a more straightforward plan which could be more directly implemented? Dr Rattray Taylor (whose posthumous book I have used as shamelessly in this chapter as Professor Paul Davies' and Dr Lovelock's in earlier chapters) has written: 'If there is one solitary fact which emerges distinctly from evolutionary studies, it is that evolution is not the execution of a consummate overall plan, divine or otherwise. There have been far too many false starts, bosh shots and changes of intention for that.'[50]

A judgment of this kind must depend on what kind of plan is thought to be required. I cannot answer for God, and we do not know the choices that are open for him; and so it is possible only to speculate. If it is God's plan to set in motion a process which will culminate in the evolution of living organisms which can reflect on the process of life and existence, and which are capable of thought and feeling, and which are able to appreciate the values of beauty, goodness and truth, and whose nature enables them to communicate with each other and to enter into personal relationships with themselves and with him, and who can make a fresh start from past errors and mistakes, then the end of the process to a certain extent must constrain its structures.

In such a case the evolutionary process and the nature of reality would have to be such that law would have to reign (or everything would be chaotic), random occurrences would have to take place (or everything would be pre-ordained) and an individual animal would have to be capable of some curiosity, purpose and initiative (or when human beings emerged there would be no possibility of personal freedom). The process would have to be such that it would tend towards increasing complexity, without which such an organism as man could not evolve. There would therefore have to be a tendency in things towards order and regularities, towards complexity and towards the evolution of intelligence and consciousness; but there would have to be autonomy within the system and freedom to evolve, so that false starts could be overcome and new beginnings could be made. God would not control this process directly. But God could have created matter in such a way that it tends to assemble itself in increasingly complex ways which make it possible to produce as its end the kind of moral and intellectual and spiritual beings which have in fact emerged.

Why is it so unacceptable that beings such as *homo sapiens* should be regarded as the end-product of evolution? Richard Leakey has written:

> I find it very arrogant that many people think that if evolution occurred, it occurred because we were to be produced – that we are the end-product, the inevitable end-product of natural selection. Nothing could be further from the truth. We are here as the result of many accidents if you like. There was nothing pre-planned about humanity.[51]

It may be that there are other beings who have emerged, with qualities similar to *homo sapiens*, somewhere else in the vastness of this universe. We do not know. But there seems nothing arrogant to me in believing that the process of creation and evolution has been set in hand to produce such creatures, for they alone are capable of conscious rational, moral, spiritual and personal activity. To say this is no way to deride or to devalue the rest of creation, but simply to state a fact.

But it is necessary to consider in greater detail what it means to be human.

7

The Evolution of Man

The ascent of man from the monkeys no longer stirs any interest. Charles Gore, the first Bishop of Birmingham, was said to be moved to despair by visiting the monkey house at the London Zoo. His successor as sixth Bishop, in common with almost all his contemporaries, is able to contemplate our remoter cousins with equanimity. However the palaeontologists are by no means so tranquil in their discussions about the way in which man made his ascent. They disagree among themselves. The discovery at intervals of new bits of bones, from which the experts appear to satisfy themselves that they can reconstruct the shape of an entire early anthropoid, always strikes the onlooker as very remarkable. There is some scepticism about claims to have found the Missing Link, even though we no longer expect modern versions of the Piltdown Man.

Among so many competing claims it seems absurd for any outsider to have his own preferred route. But there must have been some path by which man ascended, and stood erect, and used his two hands not as additional organs of locomotion but as members which were able to use missiles and learn skills. I personally prefer the suggestion of Professor Sir Alister Hardy, elaborated by Elaine Morgan,[1] that early man came down from the trees into the plains and was chased into the sea, and then emerged from the sea on to the land. Professor Hardy suggested this route for a variety of reasons. It is odd that our bodies are relatively hairless, unlike our more remote ancestors. It is odd that our vestigial hairs are arranged in a different way from those of other primates, and that they naturally lie in lines that would be followed by water as it flowed over a body in the oceans. We have kept hair on our heads, where we would have needed protection from the sun. Wading in the shallows would have helped our upright stance and searching on the sea-bed would have helped the sensitivity of our fingertips. I have recently been watching sea otters using their flippers to crack open sea-shells, and our ancestors could have learnt manual dexterity in this kind of way. We would have needed a layer of subcutaneous fat to keep us warm in the seas; and *homo sapiens*, alone among primates, has such a layer. Did we ascend this way?

This is of course speculation. However it was that man evolved from the primates, he differs from all other animals in particular ways. These centre on his intellectual, moral and spiritual faculties, especially his capacity for abstract thinking and for moral judgments, his appreciation of values, and in particular goodness, truth and beauty. Because of these faculties, human beings have a capacity for wickedness, unknown to animals. Human beings are able to communicate, and to engage in personal relationships. They have spiritual capacities which enable them to enjoy fellowship with God. Some of these abilities are present in rudimentary form among animals – whales can communicate with each other, chimpanzees have elementary powers of mind. However, the development of man's faculties of mind and spirit marks him off from the rest of the animal kingdom, and enables him to dominate the globe.

Yet our species has developed in a very short time. There was an evolutionary outburst of reptiles during the Mesozoic, and a mammalian outburst in the Pleistocene, but these seem comparatively minor advances compared with the sudden evolutionary outburst which has produced *homo sapiens*.

The physiological characteristics peculiar to man is the size of his brain. Arthur Koestler quoted from Professor le Gros Clark who wrote in 1961:

It now appears from the fossil record that the hominid brain did not begin to enlarge significantly before the beginnings of the Pleistocene, but from the middle of the Pleistocene (*circa* half a million years ago) onwards it expanded at a most remarkable speed – greatly exceeding the rate of evolutionary change which had so far been recorded in any anatomical character in the lower animals . . . The rapidity of the evolutionary expansion of the brain during the Pleistocene is an example of what has been termed 'explosive evolution'.[2]

Koestler believed that this expansion was too sudden, and maintained that as a result, there is insufficient co-ordination between the new brain and the old, quoting from Judson Herrick's *The Evolution of Human Nature* the suggestion that 'the human cortex is a kind of tumourous overgrowth that has got so big that its functions are out of normal control'.[3] Just as evolution as a whole seems to have slowed down as the advent of man grew nearer (as we now perceive with hindsight) so I hope it is not fanciful to observe that the last lap to man took place with unexampled speed.

Attention has already been drawn in the previous chapter to D'Arcy Thompson's 'grid co-ordinates'; and when suitably distorted, they show up well the transformation of the skull of a baboon into that of a chimpanzee and a man. The main difference is in the progressive enlargement of the brain case and the diminution of the jaws. As for man's brain, 'of all the organs in the body, the brain is by far the most complex. It contains approximately ten billion nerve cells or neurones, and many more supporting cells (known as glia). Each nerve cell may communicate with thousands of others, forming a network that makes the most sophisticated microcircuitry made by man seem rudimentary'.[4]

The extraordinary genetic similarity between chimpanzees and human beings has been established through molecular biology. Richard Passingham writes: 'The resemblance between non-repeated sequences of DNA in man and chimpanzee is greater than that between mouse and rat; and the average protein differs by less than one per cent between the two species. If the genetic distance is so small, why is the mental gap so great?'[5] He answers his question as follows:

The secret must lie in the brain. The brain is the only one of the human internal organs that is larger than expected for a primate of our size. It is fully three times bigger than would be predicted for a hypothetical primate of our build . . . On the index of the brain size the gap between man and chimpanzee is greater than the gap between chimpanzee and hedgehog.

How does man achieve this preeminence? At birth the brain of a baby is little bigger than we would expect for a new-born chimpanzee if it were the same body weight. Before birth the brain grows at the same rate in man as in chimpanzee and macaque monkey. But in the macaque the rate slows down markedly just before the birth, and in the chimpanzee just after birth, whereas in man the brain continues to grow at the very rapid rate that is characteristic of the foetus for two years after birth. It needs only a small modification in the control genes that direct the pace of growth to come up with a brain as large as ours.

We do not know why that modification occurred so rapidly. One cannot help wondering whether the brain of man is not in some ways similar to the horns of the Irish elk, grown too large to be useful – or rather, grown so large that it will be man's undoing unless he learns to control its use. The history of mankind shows how twisted man is, suffering as theologians say from original sin, and with a tendency to quarrel and to fight and to use his gifts for his own aggrandisement without much thought either for his fellowmen, or for his fellow members of the animal kingdom. He may well by his folly cause evolution on earth to 'start all over again'. Nonetheless the possession of a brain gives man some wonderful benefits and admits him into a far larger world of opportunity and service and fellowship.

But how does the brain of a human being differ, physiologically speaking, from the brain of a chimpanzee? It is not simply an expanded version of a chimpanzee's brain. Within non-human primates the amount of neo-cortex is related to the overall size of the brain by a simple proportion on a logarithmic scale. And this holds good for *homo sapiens*. The human cortex is just the size that would be expected in relation to a primate's total brain size. The human brain has expanded very fast, but it has done so according to the pattern of primates. (In other mammals, however, it might form only a third of the total brain compared with its actual value of 80% for our brain.)

Passingham suggests that we should be careful before claiming that human beings alone have evolved a speech area for their neo-cortex. He offers two hints how the gap between man and most of the primates may be bridged. The first concerns the two hemispheres of the brain which form the cortex. There is a difference here between man and the primates:

> In the macaque, and we assume in the chimpanzee, the two hemispheres of the brain carry out, in the main, the same functions; the task carried out by each hemisphere seems to be duplicated unnecessarily. In one experiment Richard Makamura and Michael Gazziniga at the University of New York at Stony Brook found that monkeys were able to solve a complicated problem as effectively as normal even after the removal of the neo-cortex of one hemisphere. In man, on the other hand, the removal of one hemisphere severely compromises intellectual capacity. The human brain has been reorganized so that different functions are apportioned to each hemisphere.[6]

In *homo sapiens* the dominant hemisphere tends to be the left hemisphere, and it is usually associated with speech (and therefore with intellectual) process; while the other hemisphere deals with holistic images, music, pictorial and pattern sense, and with feeling tone. As for the *corpus callosum* which interconnects them, if this is cut there is a loss of perception and loss of control over the optical field and over the hand which relates to the minor hemisphere. Speech would have produced a selective advantage, but it is nonetheless very remarkable that in a short period of two to three million years, this specialization of the hemispheres should have evolved in man. So far as I know, no one has attempted to show any kind of scenario how such an evolution could be expected to have taken place in such a brief period.

Passingham's second hint about bridging the gap between man and the primates concerns the different efficiencies with which their brains are programmed:

10.11|In its natural world the chimpanzee acquires its concepts and knowledge by interaction with the physical world. Although it can also benefit from observation of the skills and practices of its fellows, we might say that its brain is programmed by experience. The child has an added advantage; it is taught in a language.

The child too is first taught by example, but it goes on to learn concepts. Therein lies the chief difference between the two brains: man can cope with concepts, other animals cannot. The ability to speak and understand language must play a great part in this ability to comprehend concepts, since it is almost impossible to express – or even to think – in concepts without the use of language; and Chomsky has pointed out the evolution of a basic form common to all languages which seems to be the result of an embryological process in the course of which neural structures which underlie linguistic performance develop.

How did *homo sapiens* evolve this capacity for language? What kind of survival value did the earliest forms of language-expressed concepts have? Did the very complex mechanism for dealing with concepts which the human brain has evolved (and which no one fully understands) evolve by natural selection? And quite apart from natural selection, how did mutations giving rise to language occur after such a short evolutionary period of time? We do not know. The mutation rate must have been far higher than would be expected. Half a million years for this momentous development seems absurdly short. The evolution of the human brain is shrouded in mystery.

We already have amassed a long list of extraordinary functions which are said to have evolved purely through natural selection from random mutations. There are those who attempt to explain by this means the many remarkable features which man shares with other mammals; the maintenance of bodily form and functions, the development of an immune system (to which we must presumably add the production of 'interferon'), the mammalian system of reproduction, the mechanism of the central nervous system which controls the purely automatic functions of the body – digestion, respiration, circulation of the blood, composition of bodily fluids, reception and processing of input from organs of vision, hearing, touch, smell, taste and automatic control of position and movement. It seems that we may have to add to these the evolution of paranormal capabilities, and of whatever may be the as yet unknown mechanism which enables acupuncture to be a successful cure for many different kinds of illness. In addition to this long list, we are invited to add the evolution of the human brain within such a short period. Of course the human being did develop from a brain like that of a chimpanzee; but it would seem probable that other factors were at work in addition to natural selection through random mutation.

The central nervous system is a very remarkable system of its own, quite apart from its connection with the brain. The body's nervous system is built up of sensory neurons (which act as receptors of information), motor neurons (which send out information and instructions), and inter-neurons (which act as channels of communication). The input is carried by an axon which acts like an interconnecting wire of an electric circuit. The electric current passes through the cell body from dendrites, which station themselves within about a millionth of an inch from the interconnecting dendrite. When a very small electrical stimulus reaches the synapse (or junction between two neurons) a chemical substance is released which bridges the small gap between the two and thus enables the electric impulse to be passed on to the adjoining axon of the next neuron. (Neurons in the human brain are basically similar to neurons of the central nervous system.) Pulses are sent forward through the spinal cord to the brain, although some matters are dealt with within the spinal cord itself (such as reflex actions like the 'knee jerk'). The brain sends appropriate instructions back to the parts of the body through the nervous system, so that whatever action is needed may be taken.

Messages and instructions reach the brain through the central nervous system:

Nature's cabling system is an orderly one. Starting from the periphery of the body, fibres from neighbouring individual neurons are first grouped together as a nerve. In man and the other vertebrates the fibres of the nerve are sorted out on arrival at the backbone, entering the spinal column at various levels, where they join the many thousands of fibres from other levels, forming together the main cable between the output/input devices and the brain. In the human body, this main cable of the spinal cord reaches the brain with an accumulation of several million separate conducting nerve fibres. About half of these fibres are busy bringing information to the brain while the other half are busy transmitting to the muscles and glands the instructions which constitute the result of the brain's data processing and computing activities. Each fibre is a few ten thousands of an inch in diameter. Many possess a thin covering of *myelin*, a kind of coating and insulating material that increases the speed of the nerve impulse and also helps prevent 'cross-talk' among the neighbouring nerve fibres.[7]

The brain itself consists of an agglomeration of swellings and protuberances around the brainstem, with the outermost material folded up tight with lobes and folds so as to get the largest amount of cortex within the braincase. This cortex forms in animals two hemispheres, which in human beings has been enlarged to such an extent that it overlaps the other parts of the brain and fills up the braincase. The nearer any part of the brain is to the brainstem, the more primitive its function – and at the same time the more crucial.

It has been discovered, as a result of probes, that these primitive areas contain the centres of pleasure, and centres of pain, and areas where there are located sources of fear, anger and satisfactions such as come from food or from sex. Stressful situations have been artificially created in these areas so severe that monkeys have developed ulcers. 'Control centres not only for automatic physical processes that support life, but also for the essentially animal-like passions and emotions, are found in the older part of the brain that we share in relatively unchanged form with the animals.'[8]

The older part of the brain is mainly responsible for the control of these automatic physical processes. The *medulla* and the *pons* which lie closest to the brainstem are (with the *hypothalamus*) concerned for the most part with co-ordinating actions which involve the whole body such as regulating body temperature, blood pressure, heart rate and breathing; and these centres also help to maintain balance during walking when the centre of gravity alters. The *mesencephalon* has similar functions; and it also helps to regulate some of the high level activities of the fore brain. This part of the brain also monitors all the input of the nervous system and it can sound the alert when a novel or intense stimulus is registered. Parts of the older brain have connections with other parts of the brain; but these are particularly important to the *mesencephalon* because they enable it to regulate waking, sleeping and dreaming states. (Hallucinatory drugs are thought to affect this portion of the brain, and Parkinson's disease involves a disorder in this part of the system.)

Above it lies the *diencephalon* which also plays a vital part in these automatic processes. The *hypothalamus* (which forms part of it) controls the secretions of the neuro-endocrine system – a very complex mechanism vital for the well-being of the body and master-minded by the pituitary gland nearby. It is an important control centre for the regulation of the body's visceral processes which take place usually below the level of consciousness. It acts as a kind of 'chief executive' for the internal operations of the body. Next to it is the *thalamus*, part of whose function is to prepare information for and in many ways to organize the activity of the cortex. One must imagine here a busy kind of office where extracts of information sent in through the central nervous system are sent for evaluation and for comparison with data retrieved from the memory.

Many traces of memory are found in various parts of the brain; but at present it constitutes a mystery.

> We have no idea where it is. Indeed the evidence suggests that the brain's memory is incorporated into its structure at whatever point the stored information is to act. Its memory may then be thought of as distributed throughout its structure. At present we can only offer speculation as to the physical nature and detailed processes of the brain's memory . . . Our current semiconductor memory chips are inferior, in terms of capacity, but they are superior in speed and accuracy.[9]

It may be that there are different forms of memory; short-term (such as temporarily memorizing a telephone number), medium-term and long-term (including childhood memories). An analogy with computers suggests that memory may have a physical base, but the way in which learned habits persist after extensive damage to the cortex and to the 'older parts' of the brain is puzzling, and it may point towards an explanation of memory by morphic resonance (or perhaps even more direct access to the conscious self in previous states).[10]

The working of the limbic system of the old brain has been summed as follows:

> The limbic system functions in the analysis for information

relevant to the organism's needs. Thus, when we are hungry, the limbic system, in conjunction with other structures mentioned earlier, initiates a state which enables the sensory signal of food to initiate appropriate behaviour patterns, which are generated in detail by the cortex-thalamus-striatum apparatus. We experience the operation of this state of the limbic system as pleasure. When the limbic system recognizes unfavourable situations, other states are generated (experienced as fear or anger) which cause other sorts of detailed actions to be generated.[11]

The cortex is, generally speaking, where the higher activities of the brain take place. It consists of two hemispheres interconnected by the *corpus callosum*, a bundle of tens of millions of axons which bring together the neurons of both hemispheres. There are many inter-connections between the cortex and the rest of the brain. There is precise mapping on the cortex, and defined spots for visual and other sensory or motor stimuli for different parts of the body have been located. One of the more interesting aspects of the human cortex is that there is a particularly large area which refines the tactile sensations of the hands. (Similarly in pigs there is a large area concerned with the snout.) It is not easy to imagine how this area has enlarged itself so swiftly by random mutation and natural selection. It is understandable how humans with greater tactile sense might have an advantage in the battle for survival, but (if the enlargement took place gradually rather than by a saltation) it is difficult to see how it could have built up in the comparatively short time available for random mutations.

So far as the sensory and motor mechanisms of the human nervous system are concerned, the cortex is an organ of refinement and elaboration, except for the visual system which in man is greatly affected by what happens there. 'In humans, the million or so optic fibres that leave the eye spread into the 500 million neurons of the visual cortex of the brain, and this gives ample information from the retina to be processed several times over.'[12] Research on brain cells which deal with visual mechanisms have shown them to be exceedingly complex:

Most of the cells in the cortex respond only to lines of a particular orientation, between them catering for orientations at all degrees from vertical to horizontal and back. Those that are called 'simple' are very fussy about the orientation of the line – if it is 10° or 20° out they will not respond – as well as about its position . . . Hubel and Wiesel eventually revealed that each kind of cell is not distributed randomly throughout the tissue. Far from it: they discovered an architecture of columns and layers as consistent in its organization as a cathedral . . . Their conclusions, recently confirmed by developed radioactive labelling techniques, was that the whole field is mapped in the cortex in columns of cells which all respond to similar stimuli, but process them at increasing levels of complexity, and the adjacent columns correspond to adjacent parts of the visual field.[13]

Of the several hundred square inches of the surface area of the cortex a quarter is concerned with sensory and motor functions. The visual cortex is at the extreme rear, the sensory and motor strips run down the sides of the brain, and auditory areas are located at the top edge of the temporal lobe. This leaves three quarters of the surface for other uses. Half of this is situated by the front. Nowhere more than here has there been greater expansion of the brain matter during the transition from primate to man, and this accounts for the high forehead characteristic of *homo sapiens.*

This area would seem to be of paramount importance in determining the difference between the human brain and that of an animal. In fact the results seem very disappointing. The frontal lobes do appear to have some connection with a person's personality. If these are excised, or if their connection with the old brain is cut, changes appear in the personality. A person becomes listless, his old drive and energy disappears, and alteration takes place in his character. (Changes which are not dissimilar take place in monkeys which have had frontal lobotomy.) There may be a lack of responsiveness to ethical aspects of behaviour. Frontal lobotomy may relieve intolerable pain or depression, but it has in itself undesirable effects on the person. It seems as though these frontal lobes of the cortex may act as a kind of mediator between our intellectual activities and our emotional desires. They may enable us to organize our thoughts and actions to achieve our goals. They may affect our motivation. It is not without interest that damage to these areas can mean that the ability to hold together concepts or to indulge in abstract thought is diminished. They may have 'stand-by' capacity; but it is possible that these areas (rather like one of the hemispheres in the case of animals) may be useful for future development of the species.

There are in the cortex three distinct 'speech areas'. Electrical stimulation of these areas can achieve a modified aphasia, with an inability to name objects, hesitations, distortions and slurrings. Such experiments show that probes in this area can interfere with ideational speech processes. Since speech and thought go hand in hand, these particular areas must be intimately connected with thought processes. These areas are located normally in the left hemisphere (except for those for whom the left side is dominant), although severe damage to this hemisphere in early years can cause the right hemisphere to take over these functions. There is a certain plasticity in these three areas which is now becoming recognized in other parts of the cortex. Although the three areas of the cortex are all part of the same speech mechanism (and therefore must be connected up with the older part of the brain, because there is no inter-communication between the three areas themselves), they will act for one another, except that nothing can take the place of the large posterior speech area.

With respect to speech the conclusion that we all employ the same areas of the cortex must appear to us to be rather remarkable, in view of the obviously artificial and acquired nature of the function. The central integrative role of the brainstem in speech is a peculiarly satisfying discovery in view of the concept we have already developed of the cortex as essentially an organ of elaboration and refinement of functions basically controlled by the phylogenetically older parts of the brain.[14]

Yet for all the involvement of the older parts of the brain in the ability to understand language, it seems that the evolution of the new cortex is essential to its development.

How did this ability to speak develop? One can imagine that those who could communicate better could have better survival value, but it is difficult to understand how this great faculty, with its attendant power of thought, was able to evolve by natural selection and random mutation in so short a time. And why, one asks oneself, are there three separate speech areas on the cortex? Even if each area has separable functions in the organization and production of speech, it is not easy to see how a scenario could be produced which shows convincingly how these areas could have evolved unless there was a prior drive within the matter which they comprise to assemble itself in this way.

One of the more remarkable faculties of the brain is its ability to survive damage.

> Some nerve cells can survive damage, regenerate and grow back to their original point of contact, restoring functions that were lost when the damage occurred. But in higher vertebrates these do not include most of the cells of the central nervous system – the brain and the spinal cord. In almost every case cells of the central nervous system whose axons . . . are cut or crushed, degenerate and die within weeks. Meanwhile cells in the peripheral nervous system . . . can not only survive but grow new fibres along their original pathways.[15]

Although cells in the brain cannot regenerate themselves adjacent cells can form sprouts to take over the dead cells' former contacts. It is not easy to see how, on the theory of natural selection, such a mutation would have been able to establish itself. Brain damage is not likely to have been for our ancestors a common cause of death before the age of reproduction.

Another remarkable faculty of the brain is its ability to organize itself at the beginning of its development. We have already noticed the phenomenon, as yet unexplained, of cells moving about a growing embryo in order to find their correct location and relationship with neighbouring cells. Considerable research has been done in this area:

> With my colleague Shin-Ho Chung, I have been studying a particular aspect of this area of developmental biology; it concerns the way in which, in certain animals, the nerve fibres from the eye link up with an information processing centre in the brain. As will become clear, the question we are asking (and it is a puzzle common to all developmental biology) is, 'How do the cells "know" their position within tissues?' In the study of pattern formation in early embryos, the phenomenon of so-called organizers is well known . . . It looks very much as though certain cells within the diencephalon are acting analogously to an organizer.[16]

I must admit that I ought not to be surprised at anything that happens in nature, but I do find myself very surprised by this remarkable complexity of the growing embryo, and the astonishing way in which cells seem to be able to assemble themselves in the brain in the most complex way from what seems to be at the beginning just a blob of jelly. The complexity of the brain – even the brain of the primate, let alone the human cortex, is to me very remarkable indeed. I find Professor MacKay's analogy about the human cortex helpful:

> In order to form a realistic idea of the structural complexity inside your head, imagine that one cubic millimetre of your cerebral cortex were magnified to the size of a lecture hall. In this magnified one millimetre cube we might expect to find something of the order of 100,000 nerve cells. If each of these had 1,000 to 10,000 connections, each connection adjustable in ways that might be functionally important, then within this one hall we would have a structure containing up to a *thousand million* functionally significant elements. Depicted on the same scale, the nerve fibres running from the brain to other parts of your body would extend for distances up to 100m kilometres. Now let us take the arithmetic a step further. The human cortex is about 2,000 square centimetres in area, and on average about three millimetres thick. In order to complete our imaginary model of your brain on the same scale, then we would need something like 600,000 of these lecture halls, stacked side by side and three deep.[17]

It seems at first sight as though the cerebral cortex were some vast telephone exchange with a personal line, as it were, for each inhabitant of the globe, and with private personal lines linking together many subscribers. But the analogy is not very apposite. The brain is concerned with much more than mere communication, as we have seen. The mind is concerned with assessing priorities and making judgments of value as well as of fact, and also with making decisions. In so far as the process is open to observation, it appears that neurons of the brain interact with each other in a way which is either inhibitory or excitatory. Some five dozen different chemicals are said to be used in the synapses between cells to carry these messages. But more than a communication or a calculating system is needed for thought. There is need for concentration, for personal judgment in deciding on courses of action or conclusions to arguments, for the decision to make logical connections and for the ability to arrive at imaginative and creative solutions. Many of the most creative ideas have come as it were 'out of the blue' and not as the result of deliberate thought. Human beings also have feelings of 'ought-ness', consciousness of moral obligations, and the sense of personal relationship with other people, and many other thought processes, states of recollection and of creative imagination. We associate human beings with spiritual and moral qualities, differences of character. No computer can give these. It seems that the self which makes use of the material brain and which appears to be affected by it, may be in some respects independent of it.

To say this is not to deny that there are ways in which the brain does resemble a computer. Wooldridge illustrates how the *cerebellum* for example may be compared with a computer:

> An electronic computer that controls the flight of an airplane or a guided missile typically employs an equipment organization in which the detailed step by step stabilization of the flight pattern is separated from the function of overall navigational control. Stable platforms, accelerometers, gyroscopes and other equivalents of the otoliths, semicircular canals, and muscular contraction sensors of the body, are the basic input devices for computing equipment that solves the set of equations yielding the control signals for aerodynamic fins, rocket nozzle deflectors or other 'muscular' devices needed to keep the vehicle on a stable course. This dynamic stabilizing sub system appears, at the present state of knowledge, to be an electric analog of the *cerebellum* of the brain.[18]

Wooldridge gives a further account of the similarities between a computer which clarifies some of the points of contact:

> The computer scientist may well be impressed by the fact that there are several thousand such systems operating in the body, but he is not likely to be overawed by the nature of the operations involved. Feedback control systems that employ electric indications of the physical parameters of a process to provide motor signals serving to adjust these parameters to

desired standard values are an old story to him. So are stored-programme arrangements for triggering previously planned patterns of activity of the output devices. The computer scientist knows how to design combinations of circuit elements to produce these results. And, when provided with the required sensory-input and motor-output devices, he can design the circuits so that, like the central nervous system, they consist solely of large numbers of suitably interconnected simple circuit elements. At the present state of his art, the computer designer would employ electrically operated on/off switches to perform the necessary computing and control functions. The neurons of the central nervous system clearly possess the attributes which he would need for his simulation of the reflex control systems of nature, and probably some other properties if his science were sophisticated enough today to permit him to employ their additional capabilities.[19]

The similarities between computer systems and the brain and central nervous system are evident. But as I have indicated, there are great differences as well. A computer deals only in formal symbols automatically produced in response to stimulae, while a mind deals in symbols which it can interpret and understand. A computer is man-made; it is not self-assembling. It needs considerable knowledge and skill to make it. Whether or not the brain is self-assembling is a matter for debate, but the computer needs people to turn it on and to turn it off, and to supply it with software so that it can function. A computer does not do more than carry out the tasks that have been allocated to it, or the decisions it has been pre-programmed to make. A person, on the other hand, may decide to do this or to do that, and may freely use his or her will to carry out this idea or that. A person makes up his own software, as it were, either on the basis of learned behaviour or by voluntary decision. Except for automatic responses, dreaming (and perhaps day dreaming) the brain does not function without a deliberate act on the part of the person concerned. A person is not pre-programmed like a computer.

Professor MacKay, however, has used the analogy of a computer to suggest that it is a false antithesis to suggest that either the mind is to be identified with the brain, or that the mind interacts with brain function. He has proposed a third way, that the mind acts on the brain and conscious activity is 'embodied in rather than reactive with, the special re-entrant pattern of cerebral information flow that continually and actively revises its own programme and so becomes its own arbiter'.[20] But even if this were so, human self-consciousness still remains to be explained, and Professor MacKay can do no better than to assume that 'self-conscious experience is the immediate correlate of the supervisory information flow embodied in our neural machinery'. It could be; but there is no evidence to show that this is the case. The problem of self-consciousness still remains.

Those who believe that mind is identical with brain hold that consciousness is only an aspect of brain function, perhaps an epiphenomenon.[21] Evidently there is a close connection between the two. If a brain has ceased to function, a person, as we say, loses consciousness; and if loss of brain function is permanent, the person is accounted dead. Without a brain, we cannot – at least in this world – experience consciousness. Severe brain damage – or even severe concussion – can cause loss of consciousness.

Nonetheless there is no way by which biologists or biochemists seem to be able to explain the subjective experience of consciousness from the objective functioning of the brain. Although there is an evident connection between the two, it does not seem possible on rational grounds to equate the two.

The one affects the other. Professor W. H. Thorpe quotes Sperry to show that the phenomena of subjective experience interact with brain process and they can exact an active causal influence. Sperry holds that consciousness has a directive role in determining the flow pattern of cerebral excitation:

> . . . A mutal interaction is conceived between the physiological and the mental properties . . . Consciousness does do things and is highly functional as an important component of the causal sequence in higher level reactions. This is a view which puts consciousness to work.[22]

Such interaction is important, but it does not solve the problem of the origin of consciousness. Those who are materialists hold that consciousness is a kind of epiphenomenon of matter, so that a mental event is the same as a brain event. It does seem likely that human self-consciousness has evolved as a result of the increased complexity of the human brain. Since human beings enjoy self-consciousness and animals appear not to, and since human beings have more complex brains than animals, it would seem probable that consciousness is connected with the brain. But a connection is not necessarily a causal connection; and it is the absence of a causal connection which makes it improbable that the one is to be explained in terms of the other.

Sociobiologists hold that every human thought, every aspect of human behaviour, as well as every development of a human being from the moment when a human ovum was fertilized to the moment when a human being attains maturity, can all be explained as being preprogrammed and determined from the moment of that fertilization.

It would be foolish to say that this is an impossible idea; for it is certainly logically possible. But it seems exceedingly improbable. We experience freedom of thought and freedom of action, that is part of what it means to be human. To believe that all our thoughts and intentions are pre-programmed and that our freedom is illusory is contrary to human experience. It may be that this universal experience is based on a mistake or an illusion but it seems exceedingly improbable. If there is real free choice, then we are not the product of a closed system, and we are not *fully* determined by our genes.

There is a further difficulty (which has been mentioned before) which militates against the view that human beings can be fully explained by natural process. Science depends for its validity on the processes of thought. But if the processes of thought are only the epiphenomena of brain processes, this leads to a paradox. Logic would depend for its validation on physical process. It therefore loses its *logical* validity. Logical deduction would depend on a particular brain process rather than on its inherent logic. In any case quantum theory requires an observer in order that accurate measurements of subparticles can be made. 'If physics presupposes the minds of observers, these minds and their properties cannot be explained in terms of physics.'

Swinburne puts forward an interesting argument from consciousness to the existence of God.[23] Although he argues in a style very different from that of this book, I am in general agreement with his conclusions. He points out that 'one sometimes hears theologians and ordinary men saying that consciousness could not have evolved from unconscious matter by natural process'. I am not sure whether I would count in his eyes as a theologian or as an 'ordinary man' but this is certainly what I have been trying to argue.

Swinburne goes on to explore this statement in philosophical detail, which can only be summarized here. He contrasts mental events, such as thoughts, feelings, sensations, imaginings, and conscious decisions, with brain events, which are physical events within the human brain. He points out that they can both interact with each other, as when neural disturbances cause pains or when decisions cause bodily movements. He examines a materialist's explanation of these mental events in terms of scientific explanation. He puts on one side behaviourism, the view that all a person's mental events are explicable in terms of his actual or possible behaviour – a view, he says, held by few philosophers today. He concentrates on the view that the mind and the brain are identical. The materialist argues his case on the grounds that it gives the simpler solution. For him the supposition that there are mental events in addition to brain events seems to add vastly to the complexity of science without allowing it to explain anything new.

Swinburne points out the problems about such a view. It is not easy to locate a mental event – such as a concept or idea – in a particular location, that is, to locate it in the place where its particular brain event took place within the braincase. He points out the difficulty, not to say the impossibility, of deriving experienced sensations from physical properties. The materialist, however, is faced with a particular difficulty:

> To show that brain events are the ultimate determinant of all that goes on, the materialist will need to show that the occurrence of all mental events is predictable from knowledge of brain events alone.

Swinburne says that the materialist, to prove his point, would have to prove (i) that there is a correlation between each kind of mental event and one or more kinds of brain events; and that (ii) this correlation involves the latter causing the former; and that (iii) these correlations depend on natural laws simple enough to be explanatory. The first (namely that there is a correlation) might in principle possibly exist, but we could never know it, because experience is essentially private to the person who experiences it. The second (the demonstration that brain events cause experience) is extremely improbable because of our experience of free choice and free intention. As for the third:

> Brain states are such different things qualitatively from experiences, intentions, beliefs, etc., that a *natural* connection between them seems almost impossible.

The materialist would reply, I think, that there *is* a natural law linking brain states with experience, but it is not possible to formulate it 'because the basic fact of occurrent awareness seems not to be analysable into any simpler components'.

Swinburne seems to be making, by means of a philosophical argument, the same point that others like myself have made (whether we be theologians or 'ordinary people') when we say that the experience of consciousness belongs to a different category from the scientific facts of a brain event; and, although there can be little doubt about the interconnection between the two, there is little possibility of demonstrating a scientific connection between them both. If they were identical, it might make discussion simpler; but there seems no reason to suppose that they can be shown to be identical.

If the state of consciousness did not arise by scientific necessity from brain events, what are the other possibilities? Swinburne discards the idea of an ultimate dualism between physical things, states and processes on the one hand, and mental entities, states and processes on the other because this would not allow any ultimate explanation of the way things are and it would constitute 'a very messy world picture'. He argues that the argument leads therefore to the remaining possibility that these are interconnected because God has willed that this should be so.

How successful an argument is this? Mackie thinks that it breaks down because 'it depends very much on the alleged naturalness and intelligibility between an intention and its fulfilment'.[24] Mackie argues that a human being, in seeking to turn his intention into action, always has to use some exterior means which requires a scientific explanation, and that the analogy of human intention is therefore not a suitable one to explain the divine intention to connect brain states with the experience of consciousness, without providing any means of scientific explanation. However it is not always the case that a human being has to use some means requiring scientific explanation in order to translate intention into action. If I decide to start thinking out this particular philosophical problem now, and do so, there is a direct translation of intention into action without any physical mediation.

I suppose the real difference in this matter between a theist and a materialist concerns his judgment over simplicity. Is it more probable that consciousness is connected with brain events by the will of God? Or is the idea of God so intrinsically improbable that some form of causal connection between consciousness and brain events which it is not possible for us to discover is the more likely solution? For me the former is the simpler and therefore more probable solution.

The view I have been trying to put forward in this book, however, goes considerably further than Swinburne's argument from consciousness. I have argued that the self is not to be identified with the material brain. I have been trying to show that, while it is possible that the brain may have evolved through natural selection as a result of random mutations, and through no other mechanism whatsoever, this seems to me improbable. The complexity of brain mechanism in higher animals, and the degree of co-ordinated development of brain and body that must have accompanied this evolution, makes it difficult to hold that the non-human brains developed by natural selection alone. When the speed of advance in the brain from primates to human beings is considered, and the further great advances that have been made, the improbability of this seems even greater.

To what then is this development due, especially if there is no known means of affecting the genome of a living being (including that part of the genome which applies to the brain) except through random mutation? It seems likely that some directive force has been at work, either interior or exterior. It is possible that this is the presence of morphogenetic fields. It is unlikely to be due to a vitalist force, an élan vital, since there is no evidence for this. It seems more likely to be due to an inherent tendency of matter to assemble itself in an orderly way into more and more complex forms, as though the 'desire' to attain consciousness and personal relationship were built into the nature of matter itself;

and this, I shall argue later, is due to the work of the Holy Spirit within the material universe.

We have earlier considered the nature of creation, and we have noted the possibility, not to say the probability, that the big bang was not due to chance. We have considered the evolution of the universe from its first beginnings, and the precise determination of its constants, and this has further strengthened the probability that more than chance is involved. We have considered the evolution of some physical aspects of the world, in particular the constitution of the atmosphere and the oceans, and we have been further strengthened in that conclusion. We have examined briefly the evolution of life with its complexities, deviations and explosive radiations; and in the light of this the view that everything is due to natural selection working through random mutations seems increasingly improbable. And now, after this brief consideration of the animal and human brain, this conviction has been yet more strongly reinforced. And when we come to the baffling phenomenon of human consciousness, we find that we cannot see how it can be accounted for on scientific grounds by the development of the human brain; and this strengthens yet further the view that life is not meaningless but that there is an underlying purpose beyond the whole of evolution from the big bang to the evolution of *homo sapiens*.

I appreciate the unacceptability of this affirmation to some. 'The cornerstone of the scientific method,' wrote Jacques Monod,[25] 'is the postulate that nature is objective. In other words, the *systematic* denial that "true" knowledge can be got at by interpreting phenomena in terms of final causes – that is to say, of purpose.' Yet I believe that the scientific method does point to some kind of purpose in creation as a whole.

This sounds rather like the old teleological argument in a new guise. It was commonly thought that teleological arguments had been disposed of once and for all by the work of Hume and Kant. We must consider their objections before we state in a positive form the main thesis of this book.

8

Further Dialogues
Concerning Natural Religion

An Extract from the Introduction of DIALOGUES CONCERNING NATURAL RELIGION *by* DAVID HUME *published after his death in* 1779

There are some subjects to which dialogue writing is peculiarly adapted, and where it is still preferable to the direct and simple method of composition.

Any point of doctrine which is so *obvious* that it scarcely admits of dispute, but at the same time so *important* that it cannot be too often inculcated, seems to require some such method of handling it; where the novelty of the manner may compensate for the strictness of the subject, where the vivacity of conversation may enforce the precept, and where the variety of lights, presented by various personages and characters, may appear neither tedious nor redundant.

Any question of philosophy, on the other hand, which is so *obscure* and *uncertain*, that human reason can reach no fixed determination with regard to it; if it should be treated at all, seems to lead us naturally into the style of dialogue and conversation. Reasonable men may be allowed to differ, where no one can be reasonably positive: opposite sentiments, even without any decision, afford an agreeable amusement: and if the subject be curious and interesting, the book carries us, in a manner, into company; and unites the two greatest and purest pleasure in life, study and society.

Happily these circumstances are all found in the subject of NATURAL RELIGION . . .

This I had lately occasion to observe, while I passed, as usual, part of the summer season with CLEANTHES, and was present at those conversations of his with PHILO and DEMEA, of which I gave you lately some account . . .

DEMEA holds to a popular form of religion, PHILO is a powerful but deeply sceptical thinker, while CLEANTHES is more orthodox. What follows is a modest attempt to continue those original conversations some two centuries later in the same style as David Hume originally employed.

I have been reading with interest, said DEMEA, what you have written about the constitution of the universe and the evolution of the great generative and vegetative faculties of the world. It is clear that you have not, like myself, made a deep study of these matters, and perhaps the considerable wonder and surprise that you discover in yourself upon investigation of the natural world would be mitigated by closer acquaintance with it. I confess myself surprised at two particulars; first that you should, upon such slight acquaintance, determine to challenge some of the most hallowed and respected principles of those who profess such matters, and secondly that you should imagine that such speculations have any connection with discussion on NATURAL RELIGION. Indeed they seem to me to belong to a different discourse of natural philosophy, and they concern a world to which you by profession do not belong.

I myself have devoted my life to the investigation of natural occurrences, but I have been concerned with enquiry into remote particulars rather than with the discovery of a grand design in the principles and proportions of the natural world and in the mode and purport of its transmutations. A study of these subjects cannot lead our discourse towards the Object of our discussions. I feel the truth of religion, in a manner, within my own breast. I find intimations of the SUPREME BEING to whom we give the name of God not in the world of nature, but in the feelings which are generated within me and which respond to the truths found in the particular revelation granted us by the benevolence of the Deity in the teaching of the Scriptures and in the tradition of the Church. I am surprised that you have made no use of these, but have preferred rather an enquiry into matters for which neither temperament nor education seems to have fitted you.

I too, added PHILO, find myself in agreement with the difficulty which DEMEA has raised. The pursuit of knowledge concerning the mode of natural change can never bring us near to determining whether we can properly speak of purpose underlying the great spread of nature; and I had thought that it is these matters which were to be the proper subject of our discussion.

I must express my thanks to you both, replied CLEANTHES, for giving me this opportunity of explaining why I have been impelled to write these poor pages which you have read. In the first place, it does not need anyone skilled in such matters to point out some of the difficulties that attend our customary philosophy concerning the development of life. To do this it is only necessary to reflect upon some of the many learned books which explain the great variety of life that exists and has existed on earth. It is clear that Natural Philosophy cannot prove general statements about the laws of nature, such as the view that different forms of life have developed because they have been specially favoured by particular changes in the inner constitution of their being which have occurred entirely by chance. It cannot prove such a law: it can only invite that it should be tested against nature's actual occurrences. And when such a law expresses principles which cannot even be tested in principle, because such tests would concern what has happened in the distant and unknown past, then it cannot be expected to go unchallenged, the more so because its protagonists insist that this particular law of nature *and no other* is responsible for the huge variety of vegetable and animal life that has developed on the earth. It must be expected that such a law be further challenged especially when those who uphold it cannot render firm proof that any known form of plant or animal has actually been changed in this way.

The second reason for my concern with these matters does indeed concern the SUPREME BEING. You are distinguished, DEMEA, for your enquiries and researches into the world of nature; but I am surprised that you can repose your trust and faith in the CREATOR, and yet suffer it to be so unaffected by the way in which the constitution of life has actually developed. To decide that all development of the varieties of life should proceed by chance would seem a strange kind of providence in contriving the world. You might respond to me that the CREATOR would have known beforehand the full range of possibilities that chance would effect, and that he could therefore foresee that his designs would eventually establish themselves. I would in turn reply that while such a plan is possible, it would not seem to be consistent with the character of the SUPREME BEING. It would show neither wisdom nor responsibility; for if the emergence of men and women be one of the main objectives of his enterprise, it would seem unwise to leave its attainment solely to chance; and it would be irresponsible to initiate and to sustain a process over which no control can be exercised.

I think, DEMEA, that I have a respect for the foundations of religion as great as your own. But however warm be the feelings engendered in my breast, these can only be adjudged by the use of reason. In order that the mind may pass judgment upon them, it must seek for evidence of the SUPREME BEING in the world that he has made. Our own sentiments and feelings form a very small part of religion. The DEITY, unless he be so circumscribed as not to deserve that name, holds sway over the whole of creation, whether it be that inanimate part of nature, or those parts which belong to animal or vegetable life. Evidence of the CREATOR must be sought from the way in which the whole universe has developed, and, in particular, life upon earth. Without such reassurance, the feelings engendered in our hearts will be suspect. If the sceptical spirit, in others or in ourselves, is to be satisfied, the matter must be argued not by the arts of persuasion but by the strictest processes of reason.

I am glad, said PHILO, that you mention the strictest processes of reason, for I confess that I began to be afraid, when you mentioned the character of the SUPREME BEING, that you had assumed without argument that there was evidence both of his existence and of his character. While I applaud your reasons for arguing *a posteriori*, and your looking for evidences of the SUPREME BEING in the world around us, rather than reposing your faith upon *a priori* exercises of logic which appear to argue him into existence, I fear that your attempts, however well-intentioned, are not likely to result in great success. Indeed I am not as yet clear in my mind about the views which you do hold concerning the development of life from its earliest beginnings.

There are four chief ways in which this development could have taken place. It could have occurred solely by means of those changes in the genetic constitution of creatures which have happened by chance. You have told me that you reject this as the sole means of change. It might have taken place when the behaviour of animals created a need which was met in certain of their kind by the acquisition of characteristics which were transmitted (by some means as yet unknown) to their offspring. You seem attracted by certain features of this theory; and yet, rightly as I judge, you do not wish to commit yourself fully to its acceptance. A third possible reason why life has developed in the way that has actually occurred could be that at certain stages it has been willed and determined by the DEITY himself acting directly upon the inner genetic constitution of living creatures and determining such changes to happen as and when he willed. I think that you judge rightly in determining this as an unlikely contingency, as it would seem hardly consistent with the character of the SUPREME BEING to interfere from time to time with the working of his creation, as though he had created a mechanism so imperfect as to require his occasional correction.

There remains the final possibility that matter orders itself. You seem to suggest in what you have written not only that matter has a propensity to order itself in such complex ways that life emerges which is capable of repairing itself and reproducing its kind, but also that this propensity has so effected the organization and complexity of matter that a form of life has emerged which is capable of reflecting on the process itself, and even to be conscious of this reflection. You suggest that this appears to be the main purpose behind the whole process of development.

I must ask you whether there is any need to look beyond this tendency of matter to order itself. You suggest (in what you have written) that matter has been given this propensity by the work of the DEITY through the HOLY SPIRIT working within matter. Whatever this may mean, it seems to add an unnecessary complication to any account we may give. Why should this propensity be attributed to the work of the DEITY, either by impressing matter with such propensities from without by means of his transcendent power, or by working from within by his HOLY SPIRIT? Have you forgotten the words that I spoke to you many many years ago? I quote them to bring them to your remembrance:

> It were better never to look beyond the present material world. By supposing it to contain the principle of its order within itself, we really assert it to be God; and the sooner we arrive at that divine Being, so much the better. When you go one step beyond the mundane system, you excite an inquisitive humour, which it is impossible ever to satisfy.[1]

I am grateful to you, PHILO, for pointing out to me those words of our earlier conversation, replied CLEANTHES, because so many years have passed since it took place, and I am now able to define my position in a rather different way. Since you put me in remembrance of your very words, I feel that it would be appropriate for me also to cite to you some words of mine in that same conversation:

> The order and arrangement of nature, the curious adjustment of final causes, the plain use and intention of every part and organ; all these bespeak in the clearest language an intelligent cause or Author. The heavens and the earth join in the same testimony: The whole chorus of Nature raises one hymn to the praise of its Creator: You alone, or almost alone, disturb this general harmony.[2]

Since I spoke those words to you, the more recent enquiries of Natural Philosophy have given to them added force. The subtle details about which we have lately been informed concerning the way in which the universe had its origin show the wisdom of the CREATOR in encompassing his design for intelligent life to develop within it. The laws and principles under which all material particles and forces are now known to operate, and the narrow margins between which success rather than failure is the outcome of his grand design; these add to our praises to the SUPREME BEING who brought all into being. Even the very constitution of the air that we breathe and of the oceans which nurtured our remotest predecessors give further evidence of the subtlety of his plans. The availability of certain elements, in some cases only in minute amounts, show an exquisite adaptation to bodily needs which provides further evidence for the delicacy of his design.

Those who are sceptical of such a plan attribute these strange coincidences and happy concatenations of nature's laws to what they call the *anthropic principle*, maintaining that we human beings only perceive a design in nature because we happen to be the beneficiaries of its processes. Indeed we do benefit from the processes of nature, and it is true that we would not have existed had they been otherwise than they are. But these sceptics estimate the human race unfairly. They think that because it is located on a small planet in a universe whose vastness exceeds our imagination, the human race is therefore of little account within the universal process of change and development. That would be to judge the quality of a substance by its quantity. The attainment of consciousness and the development of speech and thought and the emergence of moral and spiritual faculties are of such importance and significance that we rightly regard the human race as the acme of the universal process in so far as this is known to us. If there is a plan unfolded within the process, the human race is rightly identified with its fulfilment.

These are some of the ways, PHILO, in which my earlier words have been given added force by the researches of those who are skilled in the complexities of developing nature.

I fear, CLEANTHES, replied PHILO, that you have become so carried away in explaining your own words that you have not addressed yourself to the very considerable objections which I raised against the view that you are upholding.

I had thought, PHILO, that you might suggest that I was evading your questions that you put to me, CLEANTHES responded. I do not wish to escape the rigour of your arguments. There seems to be no logical necessity to make a sharp separation between things as they are in themselves and as we perceive them; and so I judge that matter truly is ordered rather than that the mind imposes the category of order on matter. You believe that there is no need to explain the propensity of matter towards order and complexity. I do not deny the possibility that matter is naturally constituted in an ordered way. I cannot deny that there may be no explanation of this brute fact of our existence. But I ask myself whether this is the more likely explanation of its constitution, or indeed of its existence. It seems to me more probable that matter exists and is constituted in this way because God willed it to be so. This personal explanation, if it be accepted as true, needs no further enquiry or explication, any more than a personal decision by a human being needs further explication once it has been freely determined by one who might have chosen otherwise had he thought fit.[3]

Here I must admit to an alteration in my own convictions since we last spoke together. (You yourself will not find difficulty in the occurrence of such a change, since in the course of your conversations with me, you once changed your own convictions, beginning by denying that there is any evidence in the world for the design of its CREATOR, but ending by saying: 'A purpose, an intention, or design strikes everywhere the most careless, the most stupid person, and no man can be so hardened in absurd systems, at all time to reject it.')[4]

Earlier I had taken sides with you against DEMEA when I said:

Nothing is demonstrable, unless the contrary implies a contradiction. Nothing that is distinctly conceivable implies a contradiction. Whatever we conceive as existent we can also conceive as non-existent. There is no Being therefore whose non-existence implies a contradiction. Consequently there is no Being whose existence is demonstrable. I propose this argument as entirely decisive, and am willing to rest the whole controversy upon it.[5]

Perhaps the very vehemence with which I then spoke betrayed an interior reservation. Upon further reflection, I must retract some of these words, and this time take sides against you, PHILO. I can no longer say that 'Nothing that is distinctly conceivable implies a contradiction.' For there are many things which I can distinctly conceive which do imply a contradiction. For example, I can conceive of being able to know both the speed and location of a small particle; but I am reliably informed that to claim both is contrary to the laws of nature and implies a contradiction. I can conceive of a time machine which transports me backwards through time, although I am advised that, since human beings cannot travel at a speed faster than light, I am conceiving a contradiction.[6] It follows therefore that the statement 'no being is demonstrable unless the contrary implies a contradiction' is untrue. It was because I wrongly believed this to be true that I said: 'The words *necessary being* therefore have no meaning; or which is the same thing, none that is consistent.' I now retract them.

Necessary being is a phrase which is to me now both clear and simple; it signifies the existence of a being who is the cause of his own existence. It is evidently possible to conceive the opposite of this without a contradiction, because many people do conceive of a universe without a Necessary Being as its author. This means not that he cannot exist, but that he *may* not exist. I cannot take seriously, PHILO, your suggestion that the universe itself may be a NECESSARY BEING, for the matter of which it is composed can pass into and out of existence, and it seems probable that the universe itself came into being with time and space.

I have not said that I believe it possible to prove *a priori* the existence of God as the explanation of the universe. I now think that a search for proof to have been mistaken. I am looking not for proof but for probability; and it seems to me more probable that God is the explanation for the existence of matter and for its propensity towards order and complexity than the alternative view that matter exists without explanation, and that it has this particular propensity as a brute fact.

If I am forced to accept as a brute fact that things are as they are, I am denying the possibility of explaining them. But I provide an adequate reason why things are such as they are, if I conceive that they have been brought into being through the personal agency of GOD. If you ask me for a reason why God is such that he can bring about these effects, I reply that God is self-existent and has power to sustain himself in being and to do whatsoever he wills. I know that it is not possible to prove that this is so. To that extent I have not altered my convictions. But I can now say that, if God exists, he necessarily exists. I shall show you that his existence is more probable than not, not simply because this provides an adequate explanation of the existence and ordering of the universe, but also for several other causes in addition. The probability of his existence is increased by these additional causes of which he is the probable author. It is not impossible in these matters that there be other explanations; but each of these other explanations I shall show to have a lower probability in itself, and to be the more improbable because of the multiplicity of answers that needs to be given to a series of problems. A simple solution such as is provided by the SUPREME BEING is preferable to a number of different explanations of which each has not only low probability in itself but is still less probable by reason of the number of causes that they together introduce. To multiply causes without necessity is contrary to true philosophy.

I have dealt in some detail in earlier pages of my poor book with God's design in the world because if we look for evidence of his existence, it will be a strange universe which he has created for his purpose if it seems to lack all marks of any design.

I have too long kept silent, cried DEMEA, while I was listening to you explaining your more recent conclusions; but it was with some distress that I heard you speaking of personal explanation, as though the DEITY were no more than a human being. Do you continue to assert this kind of similarity between GOD and a human person? Have you so persevered in your support of anthropomorphites* that you are content to put so much weight on personal explanation? Mankind is so sunk in darkness that surely you do not wish to compare the SUPREME BEING with such evil creatures? God is incomprehensible to our natural under-standing, so that we cannot draw evidence for his existence from a comparison of his actions with those of weak and imperfect human beings. We need the guidance of revelation to enable us to apprehend what we cannot begin to infer by the mere light of nature.

I am sure that we need the guidance of revelation, replied CLEANTHES, but it does not follow that we are unable to make any inferences at all by the light of nature. We can only attempt to describe that which we cannot fully know by that which we do know. The human mind with its power of thought and of making decisions is the only mind of which we have acquaintance, and we do not demean the CREATOR by judging that he has in a more preeminent way what we humans despite our weakness and fallibility also enjoy.

Even if this be the case, said PHILO, a finite design does not bring us to an infinite CREATOR. For, if like effects have like causes, we are rather led towards a limited BEING who has designed the universe, since the elements which compose the

*This word is used by Hume to describe those who conceive of God as a human person.

design are themselves limited and finite. Moreover, there are so many seeming botches and mistakes in the design, and so many tendencies that seem to lead elsewhere than to its main purport (if the development of man, as you say, is one of the chief aims of the process), that the DEITY to whom the design is attributed seems to be minished by its attribution rather than to be praised by it.

I am in agreement, replied CLEANTHES, that there can be no proof of the infinite wisdom of the CREATOR from the consideration of his design. I have not attempted to give one. On the contrary I have contented myself with showing how *probable* it is that there is a design. I am happy to align myself with the view expressed in some words written since we last conversed:

> This proof will always deserve to be treated with respect. It is the oldest, the clearest, and most in conformity with human reason. It gives life to the study of nature, deriving its existence from it, and thus constantly acquiring new vigour.
>
> It reveals aims and intentions, where our own observation would not by itself have discovered them, and enlarges our knowledge of nature by leading us towards that peculiar unity the principle of which lies outside nature. This knowledge reacts again on its cause, namely the transcendental idea, and thus increases the belief in a supreme Author to an irresistible conviction.
>
> It would therefore be not only extremely sad, but utterly vain to attempt to diminish the authority of that proof. Reason, constantly strengthened by the powerful arguments which come to hand by themselves, though they are no doubt empirical only, cannot be discouraged by any doubts of subtle and abstract speculation. Roused from every inquisitive indecision, as from a dream, by one glance at the wonders of nature and the majesty of the cosmos, reason soars from height to height, till it reaches the highest, from the conditioned to conditions, until it reaches the supreme and unconditional Author of all.
>
> But although we have nothing to say against the reasonableness and utility of this kind of argument, but wish on the contrary to commend and encourage it, we cannot approve of the claims which this proof advances to apodictic certainty,

and to an approval on its own merits, requiring no favour, and no help from any other quarter. It cannot injure the good cause, if the dogmatic language of the overweening sophist is toned down to the moderate and modest statements of a faith which does not require unconditioned submission, yet is sufficient to give rest and comfort. I therefore maintain that the physico-theological proof can never establish by itself alone the existence of a SUPREME BEING.

With that statement of Immanuel Kant[7] I cordially concur. The existence of the SUPREME BEING cannot be proven from a study of his works any more than his character can be discovered from them with any precision. It is enough that these should point to the probability of his existence.

I see with some satisfaction, replied PHILO, that under the pressure of my questions you seem to agree that there is no place for a coercive proof of God's existence. Your study of the probabilities may however be based on a misapprehension. You seem to suppose that certain random mutations are improbable, and that because these changes in the inner constitution of creatures are unlikely to have happened by chance, therefore some other agency must be introduced. This appears to me to suggest what has been called the *statistical fallacy*.[8]

We cannot say in advance that any particular one of many possibilities would be more or less unlikely than another if the occurrence of any of them were due entirely to chance. When one possibility has actually occurred, then we can say with justice that it is very improbable that the same chance happening will immediately recur. But we can say nothing whatsoever about the degree of probability involved in its first occurrence. Any one possibility is as likely as another.

Since the inner constitution of a line of creatures may change if a particular chance alteration is beneficial to the survival of an individual and so is entailed on its offspring, the same alteration would not occur a second time *by chance* but through reproduction. Further changes would occur as a result of chance, but once again it would be a statistical fallacy to suggest that any particular change was more or less likely than another. It seems to me therefore that you have no rational cause to allege that the alteration of species through natural selection and chance alterations of their genes is improbable. Any alteration may take place with an equal degree of probability.

When you speak in such terms, PHILO, you remind me of games of chance played with cards. I am aware that there is as equal a chance that a hand of cards may be dealt containing all court cards as that a hand may contain nothing but the lowest denominations of the four suits. Nonetheless it is very rare indeed – in fact I have never seen it in all my experience – for such a splendid hand containing none but court cards to be dealt to anyone; and if it were to be dealt I would fain believe that there were some mischief afoot. And even if this were to happen once in one particular game, it would be even stranger if the same were to happen later in an entirely different game, even though *before the second hand were dealt* there would be an equal chance of its recurrence. And when I survey the whole field of change among all living creatures, there seems to have been a whole series of beneficial changes following on each other in comparatively rapid succession, far quicker than could be expected in terms of probability. More than this, there are complex alterations which seem to involve co-ordinated changes of function and which seem to take place according to some plan. In the same way there are some changes which seem to produce an organ, or the beginnings of an organ, before it is required for use by the line of creatures in which it appears. These considerations lead me to reject the statistical argument which you have put forward, and to persist in believing that changes have occurred which cannot be put down to mere chance.

I see, said PHILO, that I will not persuade you to alter your mind in this respect. But if you persist in believing that there is a designer, why do you hold that there is but one, and that he is infinite? Why cannot the universe be the product of many gods, as the ancients commonly believed before the advent of our religion? Or could you not even regard the universe as a kind of body of which GOD forms the soul, since the universe is in some ways more easily thought of as a body than a mechanical contrivance?

I do not need to spend much time, said CLEANTHES, on the former suggestion of more than one designer, since we agree that 'to multiply causes without necessity is poor philosophy'. But your latter suggestion, although it lacks some subtlety in its conception, is far more worthy of consideration. I have already agreed that it is improbable that the DEITY works his will on the universe from without, but I have made the supposition that the HOLY SPIRIT works within matter and inclines it to order itself with such complexity that it develops life, and life in turn develops into human beings. To say this is indeed to ascribe to the material universe a certain kind of divinity; and although this may seem far removed from the normal ways in which the DEITY is conceived to operate it is far more in keeping with the stricter forms of our faith than would appear to be the case. Yet we must not ascribe DEITY itself to the universe. That would imply that DEITY changes as the universe develops: that, with the evolution of human beings, DEITY comes to self-consciousness: that DEITY makes no distinction between good and evil, and right and wrong, since in the world these are so intermingled. If God exists, he is necessary being; and he brought into being the universe, whose contingent existence contrasts with the eternal nature of the SUPREME BEING. If he had created all things, they live and move and have their being in him, and they participate in a limited way in his existence; but creatures are not to be confused with the CREATOR.

I am glad, CLEANTHES, replied PHILO, that you have mentioned evil and wrong, and I will expect you later to explain how these – and also pain and want – are consistent with the design of a divine CREATOR. But I do not think that you have as yet responded to my earlier objection. A transcendent Designer could not have contrived this universe with its many false starts, its apparently useless developments, and its outdated relics of earlier epochs which still persist. To suggest a design of such a nature appears to bring the SUPREME BEING down to the level of us human beings, who are limited by being the subject of our own passions, follies and errors. Indeed the very idea of design, derived from our experience of human contrivance, suggests these human limitations.

In order to reply to your objections, said CLEANTHES, concerning an apparent lack of design in nature as the multiplicity of its forms developed, it is necessary to range over the whole of nature's panorama. I do not know (and it is not yet possible in the present state of natural enquiry to ascertain) exactly how life has developed on earth in its many and varied forms, nor to determine the exact circumstances which have made this possible.

The laws and principles which govern particles of matter, and the internal and external operations of stars (and their clusters and galaxies) seem very nicely adapted to enable a planet such as ours to come into existence and to bring life into existence. If these be effects which have happened by design rather than by chance, then the laws and fixed proportions of nature must have been fashioned for this purpose by the CREATOR. If these laws and fixed proportions be found only to be able to exist as they do at present, this would also have to be put down to contrivance; for the operations of these laws and proportions, it seems, can be traced back almost to the very moment of creation itself.

It seems that not only the formation of the planet, but also the development of its oceans and atmosphere have been so arranged that they are most beneficial for the development of life (and eventually for the development of human life.) It appears that there is a self-operating system of nature which has ensured so happy a contingency. If this be not a fortuitous happening, a cause for this must also be sought. Unless it be considered a miraculous intervention by the DEITY from without (and we have already put aside this possibility) it must be the result of an interior tendency of matter, manifesting itself in the organization of the material components of the system.

It is possible that this tendency is a brute fact of existence and we can find no further explanation; yet I have given reasons for thinking it more probable that it can best be explained through the agency of a necessary Being. If this SUPREME BEING is all encompassing, all else that exists must in some sense be within him, so that the HOLY SPIRIT is infused into the very elements of matter, enduing them with this tendency which is consonant with the Divine plan. This in no way restricts the natural functions of matter; but where there are many possibilities, and the operation of mere chance might otherwise decide, the elements naturally order themselves in accordance with this innate tendency.

I say this by way of introduction to answer your objection against the apparently poor design of nature in some of its respects; for the principles which I am upholding apply throughout the whole spread of the natural world, and not merely that restricted part of it which concerns the development of all the differing forms of life upon our planet.

This tendency of which I have spoken may be the cause why life assembled itself upon earth earlier than might otherwise have been expected, had the operation been attendant purely upon random effects. After life appeared there would have been many factors in operation, enabling it to differentiate into various forms. At no time would there have been any interference with the natural functions of its component parts in any creature. It is for this reason that the line of ascent is by no means clear and straightforward. There were false starts, long ages of little development, and certain forms of life, which emerged early, continued rather surprisingly to persist. At the same time, all was not left to mere chance, for the inherent tendency in matter of which I have spoken exercised its power in the appearance of certain beneficial mutations in the inner constitutions of creatures, so that they manifested a tendency to self-organization and complexity greater than would have been expected if all had been left to mere chance. The operation of this tendency could be described in many different ways — one of these is that of 'morphogenetic fields'.[9] I am insufficiently skilled to explain how such a tendency operates: it is sufficient to explain its existence.

The outcome of this process has been that slowly life forms have changed and become more complex. The process was influenced by many factors. It led to the emergence of the vertebrates, to the mammals and finally to the anthropoids. In no case was there any conscious choice, because the light of self-consciousness seems not to have dawned until the emergence of human beings. At times some forms seem to have been adapted before they could even be used, because of this innate tendency. It was a very uneven development, involving the proliferation of a very great number of forms of life, and what appears to be waste on a vast scale. Indeed it is only with hindsight that it can be said to have a design and a purpose. The final stages of the process which led to the development of human beings with all their special capabilities, seems to have happened with great rapidity.

At this point in the discourse, PHILO intervened before CLEANTHES could continue. I must interrupt your discourse, he said, because you still have evaded giving an explanation why a process so uncertain and uneven was contrived by an all-wise

CREATOR, if indeed there is any contrivance connected with it. Perhaps you have no reply to give.

CLEANTHES replied: You do indeed put before me problems, PHILO, to which we cannot know the answer. Since we do not share in the Divine mind, we can only speculate. We cannot know the different options which were open to him. Just as an architect, if he desires to build a house from wood, is not able to choose any design that he wishes, but must contrive a plan which is compatible with the strength and other characteristics of wood, so also the Divine Architect must choose some design which is compatible with the nature of matter and its laws, if, as I assume, God's main intention behind the whole process of nature is to enable intelligent and spiritual beings to evolve from physical nature in such a way that they are dependent upon their material bodies and yet at the same time are able to develop in mind and in character so as to fit them for their final destiny in fellowship with himself. If all that participates in existence has some intrinsic goodness, we cannot properly describe as 'wasteful' the teeming life of creatures which contribute to the possibility of human evolution.

If God wished to prepare a world in which intelligent and spiritual beings could make free choices, and in which by so doing they could fit themselves for spiritual fellowship with him, he would seem to need to create a system, from which they could emerge, which itself allows for some freedom in the operation of its natural laws. At the same time laws of nature are necessary so as to give consistency and regularity to life and to enable habits to be established. Yet a system must allow for the intrusion of chance events, so as to provide for the variety necessary for character to develop, and for creativity to emerge. If this be so, chance and freedom as well as the operation of natural law is necessary for the whole developing system from which the human race is to evolve. A system which operated purely through the effect of law and chance would not be a suitable environment from which human character could develop.

Without special revelation of the divine intention it is possible only to speculate. If there is any purpose behind the whole of existence, and if we are not the random product of a blind process, this would seem an appropriate process of development for the SUPREME BEING to have set in motion to the promotion of his grand design.

I am glad, said PHILO, that at least you have not attempted to prove such a design, but have contented yourself with speculation. There can be no positive harm in that. Proof on this matter is impossible since the world remains the same whether there is design or no design behind it: and so we can only frame theories and assess the probability that one provides the most adequate explanation. About that there are likely to be differing judgments. It would be of interest to know whether your speculation includes any room for Divine providence. For example, I am informed that the period during which the reptiles dominated the earth lasted for several millions of years, and it was only towards the end of that period that mammals made their initial appearance. Those skilled in researching for evidence about the past seem to disagree among themselves about the reason for the sudden disappearance of many of the great reptilian animals and for the ending of their dominance on the earth. Some think that a comet or small star hit the earth from the heavens, some think that there was a sudden change of climate from some other cause, while others put forward more esoteric reasons. Had it not been for the cause (whatever it may have been) might not the great reptiles still dominate the earth and thwart the design of the SUPREME BEING in creating the Universe?

I do not know, replied CLEANTHES, whether the emergence of humankind is the *only* object of this great design, but certainly it is one of the chief. Once again, you raise problems to which we cannot know the answer. If God be all-powerful, it is not impossible that he should intervene in the development of living creatures; but this, as I have already suggested, pre-supposes a design so imperfect as to need his correction. It seems more probable that he would prefer the operation of natural laws together with the tendencies which he has infused into the material components of living creatures. (I speak not here of his influence on the spirit of human beings, which is another subject.)

The history of the past suggests that the forms and shapes of living creatures seldom last for more than a certain period of time. It is likely that the period of reptilian dominance would have ended, even if its continuance had been longer. No special providence was necessary. In a similar way, if the madness of mankind were to bring to an end the human race through catastrophes wrought by human folly or by the passions of war, it is likely that in the long passage of time the processes of evolution would re-establish themselves, and mankind – or some species similar to human kind – would re-emerge later, and so the divine plan would not be frustrated.

PHILO was restive at this reply and responded by saying: I do not think, CLEANTHES, that in what you have said, you have recognized in any way that the process of development is attended by so much pain, and that human beings have to suffer so much. Nor have you shown why the Divine design seems to include so much uncertainty, whether in the matter of illness or of accidents. Why again does there have to be such regularity in the question of natural laws that these adversely effect individuals? Why do mistakes of generation occur which produce monsters, or create severe disabilities? How can you reconcile such undoubted evils with the design of an all-wise, all-powerful and benevolent DEITY, in whose existence you place so much probability?

It seems to me that your explanation of a divine design falls apart when any attempt is made to reconcile it with these grave inconveniences. If one of the objects of the process is to produce people of such maturity, of such wisdom and spiritual insight that they be fit people for fellowship with the SUPREME BEING, does not this design appear to be singularly unsuccessful in its operation? If so much energy and contrivance has been expended for so many millions of centuries on the creation and upholding of this vast universe, would we not expect to see better results than the vista which spreads itself before our eyes? A scene of pain and disaster, with millions dying from sickness, illness or lack of proper nourishment, with many people suffering malformations and disabilities terrifying in their effects, with natural disasters causing fear, terror and death, with millions of individuals engulfed in hatred and unable to communicate at any depth with one another, or lacking in intelligence and will-power and at the mercy of their passions? We see whole nations locked in conflict. The SUPREME BEING, if he exists, seems to have given to the human race skill to harness the forces of the earth but not the wisdom and knowledge to use this skill aright for the welfare of humanity. If there is a design before us in the processes of nature, surely it is a design unworthy of one whom you would wish to regard as the omnipotent and all-loving CREATOR?

DEMEA here interposed with some warmth: I have been silent a long while, he said, but I must tell you that we do indeed know the answer to all these evils, in the person of JESUS whom the SUPREME BEING sent to be our Saviour. In him we see the DEITY suffering the worst pains and insults that his own creation can give him. In him we see the supreme sacrifice which restores to people the nature they were intended by their CREATOR to have. All that which has happened in creation was foreseen, and from all eternity a Saviour was prepared who would meet the deepest of human needs, and who would put right the worst of mankind's follies and frailties, and who would remove guilt from the hearts of men. I have no patience for talk about flaws in the Divine plan. Far from flaws, it is Divine perfection which has rescued us from sin and evil, the perfect plan which we expect from the all-wise and all-living GOD.

DEMEA, after this short outburst delivered with much passion, affirmed that he would waste no more time among them, and departed from their company, leaving CLEANTHES and PHILO to continue their discourse alone in their more sober fashion.

I do not wish to deny much of what DEMEA has said with so much heart, said CLEANTHES, yet the existence of pain, evil and imperfection in the world does call for some explanation, and not merely for practical action to counter-act it. It were a strange view of the SUPREME BEING to suppose that he contrived a universe of imperfection in order to make it perfect, or that he introduced pain into the world in order to remove its sting, or that he contrived accidents in order to enable mankind to find ways of overcoming or preventing them.

I cannot give a full explanation of these problems. You know full well, PHILO, that whole books have been written on each one of them; and it would need a whole discourse on each to satisfy our minds. Even thus we could never deal fully with the subjects, because we do not know the various options open to God if he wished to produce intelligent and spiritual beings capable of free decision and choice, with bodies which have developed from the physical universe.

In some cases pain is a positive benefit, giving us warning where mere absence of pleasure would not suffice. As for suffering, although we would not wish it for ourselves (nor I hope for others), most people could bear witness to the ways in which their characters have been deepened through suffering. Nor could we feel much security in a world lacking regularities, and we should rather prefer to continue to suffer their occasional disadvantages than to live in a world where special arrangements are made in each case to meet the convenience of individuals or groups. I do not see how a person can develop in character unless he has the opportunity for freedom of decision, and also for liberty of choice in turning decision into action. If a person has freedom of choice he has liberty to do right and to do wrong; and much suffering and evil is caused by wrong choices and evil decisions. As for the sufferings of the animal creation if we impute design in creation to the SUPREME BEING we should not regard it as 'the work of a demon'.[10] All creatures have an intrinsic goodness of their own, and show a preference for life rather than death; and if predation seems bad, it is because we think of it from a human point of view rather than in the light of limited consciousness such as animals enjoy. Most animals, like human beings, prefer to remain alive rather than to succumb to their suffering by inviting death.

Nonetheless I am aware that this may not seem a full answer, PHILO, to the problems that you have raised. I would appear to have left unanswered the question you ask why God chose this particular design for the universe, if indeed he did so. It seems to me that we can never resolve this problem, because we are ignorant about the options open to the CREATOR if he were to achieve the end result for which he wishes.

If it were possible to be convinced that the CREATOR has himself suffered from the ill-effects of his own creation, then though the reasons for his choice of this kind of world remain unknown, it would not be *appropriate* to hold him in any way to blame for its attendant inconveniences. On the contrary it would be appropriate to praise him for what he has done, as DEMEA has done, and in particular for his participation within the process itself for the welfare of his creation. These thoughts however stem not from the light of natural reason but from the revelation of religion, and for this reason I mention them, for they show well the incompleteness of natural knowledge and our need for a more complete disclosure of the Divine plan.

I hope, PHILO, that my discourse has led you to comprehend the reasons why despite evil and pain and suffering it seems probable that the world, and indeed the whole universe, discloses the grand design of its CREATOR.

I claim no logically demonstrable proof for what I have put before you. It remains a possibility that what appears to be a design exists by chance only in some small part of the universe and that everywhere else, unknown to us, blind chaos exists; or again, it is possible that matter has ordered itself only for a time, and that once again blind chaos may intervene. There is even the possibility that there exist other universes than that to which we belong. We can of course know nothing of these; and we can only speak from what we do know. We cannot be expected to base our convictions on possibilities which by their nature must be totally unknown to us.

From what we do know there appears to be universal order and design, and this seems best explained as the work of a SUPREME BEING for the main purpose of developing intelligent spiritual beings capable of a free response to their CREATOR, and capable of living in relationship with him.

Although the idea of a SUPREME BEING, infinite, omnipotent and omniscient, owes something to the self-disclosure which I believe that he has made, it has been my object in this dialogue to make use of no argument which takes the form of a deduction from that self-disclosure, but rather to use it as a hypothesis, and to test its adequacy as an explanation of the universe, using solely the light of reason.

I said at the outset, said PHILO, that it would be unlikely that your efforts would be crowned with success, since you are neither a scientist nor a philosopher; and yet you trespass boldly into both territories. I cannot assess the probability of what you propose without hearing from you about those other evidences of GOD which you allege to be found in other experiences of life or in other ways of thinking.

I have spent so much time, responded CLEANTHES, on evidences for design because in these recent times they have been so sadly neglected or else dismissed out of hand. I will however seek to satisfy you in these other matters of which you speak.

All human beings enjoy consciousness and awareness, most suffer from feelings of conscience, and a high proportion have religious experience. The most probable explanation of all these experiences is the agency of God, although in every case there are other possible explanations.

In the earlier pages which you have been kind enough to read, I have written about consciousness. There are those who say that when electro-chemical systems in the brain reach a certain complexity, the subjective experience of consciousness results as a natural effect. Even if this is the case, I do not see how it could ever be proved. For there is too great a difference in kind between an event in the brain, which is in principle measurable in terms of chemistry and electricity, and an event in the mind, which is not in principle measurable, but which results in an experience of an object with colour and shape, or a feeling and emotion, or a particular concept. I do not comprehend how it can ever be possible to demonstrate that the one event is identical with the other, or that the one is directly caused as a natural effect by the other. It seems probable that the operation of the brain is required for most experiences of the mind; but there seem to be some extraordinary experiences which do not depend upon this direct connection but which seem to enter into consciousness without the interposition of the brain in any way.

The arguments of materialists, who are usually so confident, absolutely fail to surmount this obstacle which the experience of awareness places in their path. There must be some relationship between the brain and the mind. Few can accept as a brute fact a perpetual dualism which brings together the two without any possibility of an explanation. It is of course possible that there is such a juxtaposition, just as it is possible that there is a connection between the two which is capable of a natural explanation but which must remain always hidden from human knowledge; but it seems a simpler explanation, and therefore inherently more probable, that God willed this connection to exist, rather than to look for arcane causes for which no theory can be devised and no proof can be produced.

It has been said that the analogy of personal explanation cannot properly be applied to the SUPREME BEING because human persons, in translating their intention into act, always use the mediation of material means to achieve this, even if it be the muscles and ligaments of their own body to give effect to their will. It is true that no explanation by analogy between GOD and human kind can be exact because of the difference between their two natures as human beings have bodies and God does not. The relationship of intention to action in both cases is proportionate to the differences in their natures. However it is possible for human beings to translate an intention to think into actual thought without any such physical mediation, so that the analogy can be more apt than is sometimes thought.

The possibility must remain open that the brain is not always directly connected with all human awareness. There is some evidence of experiences which produce sensations and consciousness without corresponding events in the human brain. Due caution must be exercised over allegations of paranormal consciousness because it is hard to safeguard against fraud, and because the essential privacy of human experience makes scientific investigation difficult. It would be foolish, however, to regard as probable any explanation of the relationship between brain and mind which precludes the possibility of this form of awareness. The self is transcendent to the events in the brain.

And so, PHILO, you will understand why in my judgment the experience of human awareness points to God as its most probable author. There is a particular form of consciousness which we call the conscience. I think there would be general agreement that it would be illegitimate for a person not to follow his conscience. Providing that a person has taken steps to inform his conscience, it must be regarded as authoritative. A person's conscience is prescriptive in guiding his actions, and its authority for so doing cannot be properly questioned. A person's conscience may impel him to do things which seem to be contrary to his own interests, or to take action which seems contrary to the public welfare. No matter: he must obey it. So conscience cannot be confused with the fulfilment of a person's wishes, or with a sense of duty towards the public good. The very experience of conscience is to be distinguished from a desire to satisfy oneself or other people. It contains within itself a sense of moral compulsion which is unique. If it has this over-riding power, it must come from a personal source, for otherwise it would be overthrown by the person who experiences it or by the authority of others discountenancing the action contemplated.

It follows therefore that the simplest explanation of conscience is that it is the personal influence of the SUPREME BEING. All people have a diffused awareness of his universal presence and also a diffused awareness of the will of One who is all-wise and all-good. This is not only the simplest and (therefore in my judgment the most probable) explanation of conscience. It is also the way in which many people directly interpret it.

Since conscience is the awareness of a moral sentiment it is likely that its formation takes place during childhood. I am insufficiently skilled in these matters to know whether Freud's explanation of the way in which conscience is formed is likely to be correct, or whether there is any better psychological explanation. However, the way in which the sentiment is formed in no way explains its origin or its authority. There is of course the possibility that all experience of conscience in human beings is illusory and lacks authority and legitimacy, but I do not believe that such a theory is likely to gain acceptance by the generality of people: it is contrary to common experience.

People not only have an experience of conscience, but they also experience moral values. These values of goodness seem to inhere in people and situations, rather than in the feelings and perceptions of observers. Moral values seem to supervene on the natural situations in which people find themselves, and so could hardly have arisen in the normal course of events. Take for example an elderly widow giving her mite – all she has – to a charitable cause. It is not my observation that puts goodness into this situation, nor does it arise simply in the course of nature. Goodness has supervened. The simplest explanation of these values is that they are created by an all-wise God of infinite goodness. It is possible that values just 'occur' or they have their origins in the observers who perceive or feel them; but the latter at any rate seems contrary to human experience. Moral values are not the only values of this kind. Beauty is not merely in the eye of the beholder – such at any rate is the common experience of the beholder. Human love does not seem to the observer to be merely the result of glandular excretions on the part of those who experience it. It does not seem to be adequately explained by the arousal or sublimation of sexual instincts. It is commonly experienced rather as a window into a different dimension of human relationship. This, it is argued, most probably finds its explanation as the creation and reflection of God whose nature is love. As I have indicated, other explanations of these values are possible, but the simplest (and therefore the most probable) is that they are the creation of the SUPREME BEING.

Moral experience is often not far removed from religious

experience; and this is another pointer towards the existence of God.

I am surprised, CLEANTHES, to hear you say so, said PHILO. Just as moral prescriptions are affected by the climate of a particular society, so religious experience seems largely clothed in the imagery of the religion to which a person belongs. For that reason, it is often contradictory, unless all religions be true. It can even be induced by the use of drugs. Some religious experience, especially that of mystics, appears to be the sublimation of the experience of human love. It often seems to take the form of illusory happiness for those people for whom real happiness, for economic and political reasons, is not possible. Much of it can be explained through our knowledge of psychological processes. Even William James, who made an exhaustive study of the subject, could not claim for it proof of God. He would not go beyond saying: 'Religious experience cannot be cited as unequivocally supporting the infinitist belief. The only thing it unequivocally testifies to is that we can experience union with *something* larger than ourselves and in that union find our greatest peace.'[11] If you base your belief in God's existence on religious experience, I fear that your case is weak indeed.

On the contrary, said CLEANTHES, my reasoning, so far as I judge, strengthens the probability of God's existence, although I grant that it must fall short of demonstration. It is no disproof of religious experience that it is clothed in the imagery of the religion of the person concerned. The point that I seek to make is not the truth of a particular revelation of the SUPREME BEING, but the probability of his existence. That would be seen differently by adherents of different faiths. In the present confused state of natural knowledge about God, we would expect a confused medley of religious experience. Some who experience him as it were at a distance would not even perceive him as a person. Naturally there would be psychological mechanisms through which perception of him becomes possible for many, and these mechanisms, being electro-chemical, may be influenced by drugs. For some there is merely a perception of a presence, devoid of those sensations which we experience in our awareness of people, which testifies to the transcendent nature of the DEITY. There will be mistakes and illusions concerning religious experience, as there are mistakes and illusions concerning other forms of experience. But religious experience as a whole is very pervasive among all peoples. It is as common in countries where atheism is the official tenet of the state as in lands where religion is fostered by the state. Enquiries show that over a third of people, even perhaps 60%, claim some form of religious experience.[12] It is a huge claim to make, that over a third of mankind suffer from illusions over religious experience when in other ways their testimony is reliable. Why should these people not be believed? The claims of an individual may not be allowed if the person is known to be an unreliable witness, either because in the past claims made by the person have been found false, or claims made of a similar kind by others have been found false. A person's perceptions are to be judged veridical until there is evidence that they are false or unreliable. I do not believe that people would tend to dismiss all religious experience unless they had already rejected the existence of the SUPREME BEING who is being experienced. The extent and richness of this experience is very great. I am glad to cite the testimony of one who has made a deep study of this:

> There is a vast continuum of forms and degrees of theistic religious experience, ranging from the powerful and continuous sense of God's presence, experienced by the great saints, to a very ordinary and fleeting sense of the reality of God experienced by ordinary people in moments of prayer and meditation, or when reading the scriptures, or when confronted with the vastness and the mystery of the universe, or when conscious of the contingency of existence, or when contemplating the idea of God, or when aware of a transcendent claim upon one's life, or in some other context. And within this wide continuum there are also, for a number of people at least, peak experiences, unforgettably vivid moments of awareness of being in God's unseen presence. And through one's own form of religious experiencing, however intense or however faint, however continuous or however occasional and rare, one is linked to and part of a great history of religious experience. One is not alone in this matter, but a member of a great company. For some that company is the Christian church, or the Jewish race or the Muslim *ummah*, down the ages and today; and for some it is the world-wide multitude of those

who have experienced and do experience our human life as being lived in the universal presence of God.[13]

Is not the most probable explanation of this religious experience the presence of God himself? If there is a God, would it not be strange that no one should have any experience of him? Of course it is possible that this vast range of experience is all based on various illusions and delusions, but it seems to me the simplest explanation, and the more probable one that it is based on the existence of God.

Finally, PHILO, I put before you a last consideration which corroborates what I have previously affirmed. The concept of DEITY seems to be a basic need of mankind. It is in the nature of human beings to worship someone or something. If they do not worship the SUPREME BEING, they substitute idols. To worship material objects is to regard them as superior to human beings, which is absurd. To worship a fellow human being or some of his or her attributes does not satisfy the deepest needs of mankind. I would even regard much of the current restlessness and frustrations which so many people exhibit as the result of their living in a secular society with a diminished belief in or an actual denial of GOD. Human beings, in order to achieve their potential, seem to need the challenge and the strengthening, the forgiveness and the self-acceptance which it is the good pleasure of the SUPREME BEING to give them. They need faith, hope and love which come from a transcendent source.

I have long been silent while you spoke, PHILO here interrupted with some warmth, but here I must interpose two objections to which you must respond. First, the practice of religion has at times brought out not the best but the worst in man. Secondly, if what you say is true, then belief in GOD may have been 'bred into' mankind, for it should make him fitter to survive in the competitiveness of life, and those with such belief are more likely to survive to pass this on to their offspring. The existence of a real need for God in no way demonstrates his actual existence.

I am delighted, replied CLEANTHES, that you have given me the opportunity to comment on these matters. I cannot deny that terrible things have been perpetrated by human beings on one another in the name of God. I believe it to be the case that the good far outweighs the bad in this matter; but human beings have the capacity to corrupt the best into the worst, and at times they have done this. I can only reaffirm that human beings do require a belief in God to meet their deepest needs and to achieve their highest potential. Nor can I deny the evidence of my own eyes that those who have belief in God, do often surpass others in the race of life. I note, however, that religious parents do not always have religious children, and that many who are most deeply committed to the SUPREME BEING come from homes where there is no belief in God.

I agree with you warmly when you say that our need for God does not necessitate his existence, and I would never wish to claim that this is so. All that I affirm is that, if God does indeed exist, we would expect human beings to have need of him. This I believe to be the case. I have spoken to you about the human need for God not because this proves his existence, but because it corroborates the earlier indications that I have given you that it is indeed far more probable that God exists than the contrary. The various points that I have made need to be taken not in isolation but as a whole, in order to consider whether they hold together and support one another. In my judgment they form together a case which falls short of apodictic proof but which can rightly be claimed to have very high probability indeed.

I am grateful to you, PHILO, for enabling me to expound to you at greater length my explanation of the reasons why it is so very much more probable that God should exist than that he should not. I understand by God that infinite BEING, all-wise, all-powerful, all-loving, perfectly free and self-existent. I have spoken to you about the existence of matter, about the development of matter and of life, and about its evolution until *homo sapiens* emerged. I have spoken with you about man's awareness, about his conscience, about the existence of moral values and about religious experience, and his need for God. Of all these God seems to me the simplest explanation. I have considered other possible explanations in every case, and explanations which do not involve God remain open possibilities. But it seems to me that God is far the most probable of all explanations.

In the first place, he is the simple and adequate explanation of all the puzzling matters of which we have spoken in this dialogue. In each matter which we have discussed, different explanations are possible. But it is more simple to have one explanation for all, and in each case God, it seems to me, provides the simplest explanation, as well as being himself simple in nature. (If it were said that the simplest explanation of all is the solipsist that I alone exist, I would reply that that is not a sufficient explanation, since I am not a necessary being.)

If God exists we would expect him to make himself known to us in guiding us to right action (and he has done that through conscience). We would expect him to make himself known to us as a presence (and he has done that for many through religious experience). We would expect him to make himself known to us by the works that he has done (and he has done that through creation). We would expect some impress of his nature in his works (and we find that in moral values, in beauty and through love).

We would expect him also to give us some assurance that he has a design for his universe, as well as to make known to us some outline of his purpose and plan. These can be seen in the creation of the universe, and in the development of matter and of life in the world. I have spent much time in attempting to examine how modern enquiry enables us to see better this plan, because this is commonly denied by many who are professionally concerned in researches in Natural Philosophy. Indeed it is important for me. I would have to revise my own idea of the SUPREME BEING if it could be demonstrated that he created the universe without any design, and left the emergence of mankind to blind chance. That I do not consider to be probable either from the nature of the evidence concerning the development of the universe, nor from the light of reason.

And now PHILO I have talked overmuch. When we talk again you must explain yourself as fully as you wish, unless my closing discourse has convinced you of the reasonableness and indeed the probability of the SUPREME BEING.

9

The Concept of Divine Immanence

The earlier chapters of this book have been concerned with
evidence for the probability of God. The question that now
remains to be asked concerns theology rather than the natural
sciences. To what extent are the ideas of God that have been
suggested in the earlier parts of this book compatible with
traditional theism, and in particular with traditional Christianity?

John Henry Newman described God as theists believe him to
be:

I speak then of the God of the Theist and of the Christian: a
God who is numerically One, who is Personal; the Author,
Sustainer and Finisher of all things, the life of Law and Order,
the Moral Governor; One who is Supreme and Sole; like
Himself, unlike all things beside Himself which all are but His
creatures; distinct from, independent of them all; One who is
self-existing, absolutely infinite, who has ever been and ever
will be, to whom nothing is past or future; who is all perfection
and the fulness and archetype of every possible excellence, the
Truth itself, Wisdom, Love, Justice, Holiness; One who is all
All-Powerful, All-Knowing, Omnipresent, Incomprehensible.
These are some of the distinctive prerogatives which I ascribe
unconditionally and unreservedly to the great Being whom I
call God.[1]

This appears to describe God in such a way that he is absolutely transcendent over all his creation. What kind of contact could such a God have with an evolving universe? Since he is said to be 'personal' (whatever that phrase may mean when applied to God), he may be presumed to have personal relationships with human beings of some kind; but hardly with inanimate nature. He is said to be 'Author, Sustainer and Finisher of all things', as though these words should define his whole contact with the universe, ordering what is to be, creating and maintaining it in being. Such a view which understands God purely in transcendent terms has been very common. It is not, however, in accord with traditional Christian theology.

The Hebrew word *ruach* was used both for God's Spirit and for breath, which was probably the way in which the direct influence of a very personal God was thought to operate. God's Spirit is involved in the very start of creation (Gen. 1.2).

> Out of those depths of undifferentiated chaos all the multitudinous forms of existence are going to be beckoned into being by call and response. But in that timeless moment nothing is present except the ardent cherishing love, the irresistible will for communion, of the Go-Between God.[2]

The breath of God is not merely the agent of the moment of creation itself, but also the agent for sustaining that creation (Ps. 104.30). His Spirit not only renews the face of the earth, but is also responsible for the creation of man. 'And the Lord God formed man of the dust of the ground and breathed into his nostrils the breath of life; and man became a living soul' (Gen. 2.7; cf. Job. 27.3; 33.4). This dynamic Hebrew idea of God's Spirit was later fused with Greek thought, so that the author of the Wisdom of Solomon, influenced no doubt by Stoic ideas, sees the Spirit of God in all things. 'The Spirit of the Lord fills the whole earth' (Wisdom 1.7) he writes, and again 'Thy imperishable breath is in them all' (Wisdom 12.1). This is to be paralleled in earlier tradition in the words of the psalmist:

> Where can I escape from thy spirit?
> Where can I flee from thy presence?
> If I climb up into heaven thou art there;
> If I make my bed in Sheol, again I find thee.

> If I take my flight to the frontiers of the morning,
> or dwell at the limit of the Western sea,
> even there thy hand will meet me
> and thy right hand will hold me fast (Ps. 139. 7–10).

A function similar to that of the Spirit was ascribed both to divine wisdom and to the divine Word, and a cosmic significance is assigned to the Wisdom of God in Prov. 8.22ff., Wisdom 1.7, 12.1.

In the Old Testament the concept of the divine Word was dynamic, the voice of God giving effect to the divine will. 'By the Word of the Lord were the heavens made' (Ps. 33.6; cf. Ps. 50.1). To this Jewish idea of the Word were added Hellenistic ideas of Reason, combined in the same Greek word *Logos*. The beginning of this fusion of ideas can be seen in the New Testament. 'The Word, then, was with God from the beginning, and through him all things came to be; no single thing was created without him. All that came to be was alive with his life' (John 1.2f.). The pre-existent Christ was identified with the Logos, so that Paul could write, 'The whole universe has been created through him and for him. And he exists before all things and all things are held together in him' (Col. 1.16). The early Greek Fathers were preoccupied with this concept of the *Logos*, both as the rational expression of the godhead and also as the agent in creation. This led to the comparative neglect of the parallel concept of the Spirit.

Nonetheless both Word and Spirit, as we have seen, were part of the early Christian tradition. The implication is clear. God's universal presence is everywhere. This has been eloquently described by Dr John Taylor.

> If we think of a Creator at all, we are to find him always on the inside of creation. And if God is really on the inside, we must find him in the processes and not in the gaps. We know now there are no gaps, no points at which a special intervention is conceivable. From first to last the process has been continuous. Nature is all of a piece, a seamless robe. There is no evidence of a break, as we once imagined, between inorganic matter and the emergence of the first living organisms; nor between man's animal precursors and the emergence of man himself. If the hand of God is to be recognized in this continuous creation, it must be found not in isolated intrusions, not in any gaps, but in the very process itself.[3]

H. B. Swete comments on the New Testament evidence: 'The conception arose that the Word and Wisdom are the two Hands of God, instruments of creative activity which are not external to the Godhead, but inherent in It.' He continues:

> It was not however only in the original creation of the world that the ancient Church saw the handiwork of the Spirit; the immanence of the Creator Spirit in the world that He had made was also clearly recognized. The Church read in her Greek Bible that 'the Spirit of the Lord hath filled the world' and 'holdeth all things together'; and 'Wisdom reacheth from one end of the world to the other with full strength, and ordereth all things graciously'; and she applied all this to the hypostatic Spirit of the Holy Trinity. 'The Spirit', writes John of Damascus, summing up the teaching of the fourth century, 'is creative, all-ruling, all-working, all-powerful, sovereign over every creature, partaken of by every creature, and by Himself creating and being given to all things, sanctifying and holding them together.' 'He fills all things with His essence, and holds all together: he can fill the world with His essence, but the world itself cannot set bounds to His power.'[4]

Thus in the early church God was not merely understood as transcendent, but also immanent throughout his creation. Such teaching was not unique to Christianity. According to the author of the Acts of the Apostles, Paul, when speaking to the Athenians from Mars Hill, spoke of God in this way, appealing to the religious conscience of his hearers: 'They were to seek God and it may be to touch and find him; though indeed he is not far from each one of us, for in him we live and move and in him we exist; as some of your own poets have said, "We are also his offspring"' (Acts 17.27).

In traditional orthodox theology God is transcendent because he is not himself involved in the mutability and contingency of his creation. His immanence is understood by his involvement in creation 'by essence, presence and power' (to use the scholastic phrase), without which his creation would collapse into nothingness, or 'fall to naught for nothingness' as Julian of Norwich puts it.[5] So God is both transcendent to his creation and immanent within it. All being, as we know it, participates in the infinite Being of God. E. L. Mascall quotes Fr E. Przywara on this relationship of the analogy of being: God 'as the pure "Is", is on the one side so inward to the creation that the transient "is" of the creation is only *from* him and *in* him – and yet, on the other side, differentiated from his creation, above it as the pure "Is", for whom no relationship to anything which is "becoming" is in any way possible.'[6]

The 'analogy of being' was denied in much Protestant theology. The fallenness of creation through the sin of Adam was usually regarded as so great that the point of contact between God and his creation had been lost and needed to be re-created; and this was achieved, according to Protestant theology, through the atonement of Christ. Catholic theology, however, continued to insist on both the immanence and the transcendence of God, so that grace perfects nature but does not destroy it.

The advent of developmental ideas altered the perspective in which immanence is to be understood. Previously the world was regarded as a static creation, made by God in accordance with the account in Genesis. However, when it began to be realized that these stories are religious myths, and when the result of scientific enquiry showed a gradual process of development from earliest beginnings, this presented a challenge to theologians to re-think their doctrine of immanence. To what extent, if any, was God involved in the development of his creation?

J. R. Moore recounts the reaction of theologians to Darwinism. Here is his account of Anglo-Catholic theology typified by A. L. Moore and Charles Kingsley:

> The Christian doctrine of God, he (Moore) believed, does indeed reconcile science and faith, but not by sacrificing morals to a one-sided emphasis on the divine sovereignty. Rather the reconciliation comes in a fresh appreciation of God's triune nature and a 'fearless re-assertion' of 'the old almost forgotten truth of the immanence of the Word, the belief in God as "creation's secret force"'. No less a doctrine will accommodate both Darwinism and theistic belief. 'Slowly and under the shock of controversy,' said Moore, 'Christianity is recovering its buried truths, and realizing the greatness of its rational heritage'... Moore's re-assertion of orthodox theology was

truly 'fearless'. 'Either God is everywhere present in nature', he declared, 'or He is nowhere ... We must frankly return to the Christian view of direct divine agency, the immanence of Divine power in nature from end to end ... or we must banish him altogether.' The same boldness, the same fearless statement of theological alternatives in the face of Darwinism, was characteristic of another prominent Anglican clergyman, Charles Kingsley ... Kingsley pointed out that scientists 'find ... they have got rid of an interfering God ... (and) have to choose between the absolute empire of accident, and a living, immanent ever-working God'.[7]

This identification of the immanent working of God with the evolution of the cosmos tended to fall away as the implications of Darwinism – and later neo-Darwinism – sank into the minds of theologians. There are those who seem to have, as it were, retreated to the earlier scholastic view that God is merely present in his creation by 'essence, presence and power'. So Peacocke writes of divine immanence:

> God is in all the creative processes of his creation, and they are all equally 'acts of God', for he is everywhere and all the time present and active in them as their agent. They *are* his acts and he cannot be more or less present in some acts rather than others, for he is not, as it were, a substance diffused through the cosmos more concentrated at one point or time than at another. All this is what we mean by saying that the Creator is *immanent* in his creation, and that is why we look for his 'meanings' (his intentions, proposals and purposes) *within* the world of which we are part.[8]

I find this statement hard to combine with the neo-Darwinism the author seems to espouse.

Maurice Wiles seems to agree with Arthur Peacocke here. 'I have argued,' he writes, 'that the idea of some special relationship of God to particular events is not to be excluded in advance as logically absurd. But logical possibility is not sufficient by itself to justify positive affirmation. Nor do I think that such a positive affirmation can in fact be justified.'[9] Wiles admits that this view is deistic in so far as it does not claim any effective causation on the part of God in relation to particular occurrences, although he believes that it does full justice to most religious experience. It seems to me that such a view, if it accepts the neo-Darwinist approach (and certainly it puts forward no suggestion of other approaches) leaves the emergence of human beings to random events and denies Divine providence, unless it be said that God in his omniscience foresaw the result of all random occurrences. It seems to leave God merely as 'the ultimate source of all existents'.[10]

William Temple pointed out the different attitudes engendered by science and religion in this connection:

> The only way to hold together a vital religion and a scientific apprehension of the world is to assert some form of Divine Immanence. We do a great disservice alike to philosophy and to religion, if we minimize the divergence of the tendencies proper to science and to religion at this point. Because science works with uniformities it is unable to allow in its own processes for any variability in nature; and it is not easy for the man of science to admit that such a variability may be real, even though science can take no account of it. Similarly because religion is concerned with Divine Personality it must assert the variability of a natural order which is the expression of that Personality, though for such variation, as for constancy, there must be 'sufficient reason'.[11]

And so we are left with the need for divine immanence if there is to be any reconciliation between science and religion. But how is that immanence to be conceived, especially in a universe governed, we are told, mostly by the combination of natural laws and chance? It is one thing to assert that 'it is by the Holy Spirit that grass grows and trees bring forth leaves and flowers and fruit, that birds fly and fishes swim, that engines turn and trains and cars and aeroplanes go their way'.[12] But it is another to define precisely what is meant by the Holy Spirit; whether this is merely a synonym for the flow of energy that maintains the world in being, or whether the work of the Holy Spirit is to be seen in the way that the created universe develops. If so, how does he cooperate with the creation itself?

The view put forward in this book is that God is present within his universe, and he upholds and sustains it in being as well as creates it. Indeed his upholding of the universe is a kind of continuous creation. This is the traditional view of divine immanence. However, greater meaning here is given to divine immanence than this. God's Spirit is leading the development of the universe to greater complexities until conscious mind emerges in human beings. This has been well expressed by Dr John Taylor:

> As a believer in the Creator Spirit I would say that deep within the fabric of the universe, the Spirit is present as the Go-Between who confronts each isolated spontaneous particle with the beckoning reality of the larger whole and so compels it to be related to others in a particular way; and it is he who at every stage lures the inert organisms by giving an inner awareness and recognition of the unattained.[13]

Dr Taylor earlier quotes from Charles Birch to make clear that in using words such as 'awareness' or 'recognition' he is not referring to consciousness but using anthropomorphic terms as a model by which to express the tendency towards order and unity and complexity which are in the nature of things.[14]

It has been suggested that, while natural selection accounts for many aspects of evolution, it is not the sole explanation. Although there is no external force imposed on species, and in particular on their genetic systems, mutations occur which would not be expected by random mutation. This is not because of external pressure, but because of the bias implanted in matter. Such bias is not, of course, to be detected by scientific measurement (and so the hypothesis is not testable) since there is no possibility of setting alongside it matter which is not implanted by this bias towards complexity and integration. Another way of describing this bias would be to call it the Holy Spirit working within the matter of the universe, unfolding the purposes of the Creator by immanent operation. W. R. Matthews describes it thus:

> The activity of the Spirit may perhaps best be expressed in the most general terms, as that *nisus* in things and in persons which seems to drive them forward towards a higher degree of perfection. As we have seen, the idea of a *nisus* of this character is not foreign to modern philosophies of evolution. Alexander and Bergson in their different manners, and the New

Idealists have recognized a tendency in the natural world towards higher types and states of existence. It has been widely admitted that here the philosophy of evolution seems to hold out a hand to the Christian belief in the Holy Spirit. But it is not always seen that the Christian doctrine of the Trinity has one great advantage over the pure doctrine of the immanent life-force of the *nisus* in things. It has a basis for the idea of value, for the conception of 'higher' and 'more perfect'. In the words of the prayer, 'all things are returning to perfection through Him from whom they took their origin' – they are moving towards the Creator.[15]

This concept of a *nisus* in things must be clearly distinguished from Bergson's concept of *élan vital*. He wrote in *Creative Evolution*:

Life as a whole, from the initial impulsion that thrust it into the world, will appear as a wave that rises and which is opposed by the descending movement of matter. On the great part of its surface, at different heights, the current is converted by matter into a vortex. At one point alone it passes freely dragging with it the obstacle which will weigh on its progress, but not stop it. At this point is humanity; it is our privileged position . . . On flows the current, running through human generations, sub-dividing itself into individuals.[16]

Bergson's semi-gnostic view of life and matter suggests a special vital characteristic. Vitalism, as the name implies, suggests a directive tendency which is peculiar to life, whereas the hypothesis put forward here is not confined to vital processes, but applies to the whole of cosmic evolution. Henderson writes: 'it is conceivable that a tendency could work parallel with mechanism without interfering with it'; and it is this which I am suggesting.[17]

Process theology has taken on board some such concept by the distinction made by its theologians between God's primordial nature, which is transcendent, and his consequential nature, which changes and 'becomes' in loving response to other entities about him. 'He is the great participant, with his creatures, in the affairs of nature-history, and this does not leave him unmoved or unchanged. Thus, just as the universe is becoming, so is he.'[18] I do not intend to pursue this line of thinking here, because, while the distinction between the two natures of God seems reminiscent of the Eastern patristic tradition of the 'essence' and the 'energies' of the godhead, it is used in a different context which does not seem to do full justice to the transcendence of God, but inclines so much to his immanence as to call into question his eternal and necessary being.

The best phrase by which the balance of immanence and transcendence as suggested here can be described is 'panentheism'. According to the *Oxford Dictionary of the Christian Church*, panentheism is 'the belief that the Being of God includes and penetrates the whole universe, so that every part of it exists in him, but . . . that his being is more than, and is not exhausted by, the Universe'. This view does not imply that God 'needs' a physical universe, as process theology sometimes seems to suggest, but that he determined to create a physical universe in order to achieve his purpose in the emergence of people capable of responding to his love. It is expressed in scripture eloquently in the words of Ecclesiasticus:

> The sum of our words is, He is all,
> How shall we have strength to glorify him?
> For he is himself the great one above all his works
>
> > (Ecclus. 43 276–28).

The same thought is contained in a gloss in a ninth century Latin manuscript belonging to Cambridge University Library which comprises the earliest extant writing in the Welsh language:

> The world cannot express thy glories, O true Lord.
> Even if the grass and the trees were to sing . . .
> Letters cannot contain them, letters cannot express them . . .
> He who made the wonder of the world will save us,
> has saved us,
> It is not too great toil to praise the Trinity.
> It is not too great toil to praise the Son of Mary.[19]

Teilhard de Chardin was a major proponent of panentheism:

> In order to take possession of me, my God, you who are so much more remote in your immensity and so much deeper in the intimacy of your indwelling than all things else, you take to

yourself and unite together the immensity of the world and the intimate depths of my being.[20]

In *Le Milieu Divin* he speaks of the 'diaphany of the Divine at the heart of the universe', and in *Hymn of the Universe* of 'that which in everything is above everything'.[21] Teilhard made clear (for example, at the end of *The Phenomenon of Man*), that he was not a pantheist, because he believed in the transcendence of God; but at the same time he believed that all things exist in God. In the light of the biblical testimony to the immanence of the Word and of the Spirit within the created universe, and in the light of patristic thought, Dr J. A. T. Robinson was surely right in his claim that panentheism is 'what traditional theism has always sought to represent. There is nothing new or unorthodox about it. The only question is whether the classic projection of theism can for most people today succeed in expressing it. In the *content* of what it is affirming panentheism stands nearer to theism. Part of the difficulty is that the *word* sounds very much nearer to pantheism.'[22]

The poets seem to be able to describe the *nuances* of panentheism better perhaps than the philosophers. Gerard Manley Hopkins wrote:

The world is charged with the grandeur of God.

He goes on:

There lives the dearest freshness deep down things;
And though the last lights off the black West went
Oh, morning, at the brown brink eastwards, springs –
Because the Holy Ghost over the bent
World broods with warm breast and with ah! bright wings.

Alexander Pope wrote:

To him no high, no low, no small;
He fills, he bounds, connects and equals all.[23]

Wordsworth, in his well-known lines on *Tintern Abbey*, spoke of a 'sense sublime of something far more deeply interfused'. It is easy to slip from this into the worship of nature, but panentheism calls rather for the worship of God in nature. Helen Oppenheimer writes of the relationship of God to matter thus:

Of course God has a 'primary relationship' with physical reality; He created it. Nothing could be more primary than that . . . Without claiming to understand either infinity or creation one can then move on to say something like this: just as God has an infinite and not a particular point of view, so He has a peculiar and mysterious relationship, as it were like 'animating' but more so, with *every* cluster of matter. Such a conception does not sink God in the world. It is technically panentheism rather than theism.[24]

It seems to me, therefore, that the immanence of God in his creation, of the kind that I have tried to outline in this book, is wholly consonant with the traditional doctrine of God, and it seems to be consonant also with the phenomena of the evolutionary process investigated in the natural sciences. We are being given this century a deeper understanding of the Holy Spirit. God is not only the creator, upholder and sustainer of all that is, but all being participates in his being, and his glory is to be seen in the smallest particle of matter as well as in its evolving forms.

IO

The Probability of God

The time has come when I must try to draw together the threads of my thinking about the probability of God, with special reference to the so called argument from design as it looks in the light of the contemporary scientific scene.

Preparing to write this book, and its actual composition, has been like a personal adventure into an unknown country whose language I cannot properly speak.

I was educated on classical literature and theological studies, and I first heard tales about this country many years ago on the High Table of Caius College, Cambridge when I was Dean there. The stories I was told whetted my appetite to visit it.

In the years that followed, I always read with particular interest any tales that I came across about it. These continued to fascinate me, so that I had to watch myself, or I would steal time from my work to read about it. The time even came when I began to make my own collection of other people's stories about this fascinating country.

The more I read about it, the more I felt mistrust of the usual guide books which are published about this land, and how it came into existence to develop in the way it has done. Finally, this unknown land cast such a spell upon me that I was forced to leave my ordinary work, and venture forth to visit it – as I have done during my recent spell of sabbatical leave. The visit was enthralling and fascinating. It led me to realize how little I know about that country, and how ill-equipped I am to write about it. Anything that I could describe would be of interest not because I am an expert traveller, or a knowledgeable writer of travel books, but rather because I am an amateur giving my honest impressions, and attempting to describe what I feel to be the real *ethos* and underlying values of the land, so different from those which experts usually describe.

And so at the end of this book I summarize my impressions. So far as the unknown country is concerned, it is far more beautiful and far more complex than I had realized. The advances of knowledge in every branch of the natural sciences, and the exponential increase in our understanding of the universe, from its smallest constituents to its most complex forms of life, within a very short period of time, has been truly astounding. No less astounding to me at least is the complexity of nature and its interrelatedness. I have had to learn the lesson that reactions at a microscopic level can have macroscopic results.

The huge accumulation of scientific knowledge has been the outcome of increasing specialization in particular scientific fields. This has reached such a degree that it is quite impossible for one person to be expert over the whole field of the natural sciences, and although specialization pays dividends in advances of knowledge, there seems to be a debit in the lack of integration of scientific knowledge.

The problems of specialized investigations are so great that scientists find that their energies are for the most part taken up with investigating what happens and how, so that they seldom have time (or, it must be admitted, the interest) to ask themselves how the object of their investigations originally developed and evolved.

Science, the ordered investigation of the natural world, is quite a different discipline from the philosophy of science, which is concerned with its assessment in terms of meaning and interpretation. Most scientists, bred on the dogma of Darwinism, assume that (if they are investigating matters concerning living organisms) the object of their investigation evolved by natural selection of random genetic mutations. The general acceptance of this (to me largely improbable) dogma is one of the stranger aspects of the scientific scene.

I believe that the dogma has for scientists some natural

attractions. Most scientists carry out their work by means of a series of physical measurements of one kind or another. Such a method of procedure inevitably influences their presuppositions in favour of a material solution to scientific problems. This is provided by neo-Darwinism.

Other scientists, such as cosmologists and physicists, may be concerning themselves with areas too small (or too distant) for physical investigation. They are therefore dependent upon theory, usually mathematical theory. The fascination of complex mathematical theory can, I believe, lead to dubious presumptions. There seems to me an inclination to suppose that what is mathematically possible necessarily provides the correct interpretation of a problem. There is a logical fallacy here. What is mathematically possible is only mathematically possible. It may provide a correct explanation – and it may not. Other facts in the total situation must also be weighed before a professional judgment is made.

There is a natural disinclination on the part of any scientist investigating any phenomena to ascribe the solution of any scientific problem to divine operation. This would mean the end of scientific investigation, the end of a scientist's work. It would be a damper on scientific curiosity. The ascription of divine agency to any natural phenomena seems outside the proper province of a scientist. His concern, as a scientist, should be only with continuing investigation.

The arguments for the existence of God certainly lie right outside the province of the natural sciences. The only such 'argument' that has any connection with the sciences – because it is the only argument which is concerned with material entities themselves – is the so-called argument from design.

Any attempt to prove the existence of God by means of reasoned argument has failed, and will always fail. God cannot be argued into existence, if he wishes his creatures to approach him in faith rather than in the certainty of knowledge.

One of the more unfortunate results of attempts to prove the existence of God has been that the successful demolition of these proofs has been generally understood as disproving his existence, and showing that he does not exist. But this is not the case. All that has been achieved is uncertainty about the matter, which is very different. The question remains open.

I do not believe that the so-called 'ontological argument' proves that God exists. Properly stated, however, it is important for it shows us something of the range of explanation that God can provide, and it also makes clear that, if God exists, he is necessary self-existent Being.

The question can only be rationally resolved by a considered judgment concerning the balance of probabilities. It is likely that these probabilities will be assessed differently by individuals according to their presumptions and prejudices.

In this book I have devoted one short chapter to a consideration of the idea of 'immanence' in Christian theology, and I have assumed that the God of Christian theism provides a possible explanation to the phenomena of existence. But I have tried, so far as I can, to state the case fairly.

I cannot deny that the possibility that there is no God remains open. The important question is – how probable or improbable is it? *It seems to me, on as balanced a judgment as I am capable of making, exceedingly improbable.* In this concluding chapter I shall attempt to justify this sweeping statement.

The appearance of matter and energy at the big bang may be due to the direct agency of God, or may have been brought into existence by natural causes as yet very imperfectly understood. It is possible that these natural causes are themselves inexplicable, a 'brute fact'. In my judgment the view that they find their explanation in the personal will of God is more probable, but needs further support. I find this support partly through some very remarkable coincidences in the constitution of the universe which have made it hospitable to life.

The distribution of gas in the universe from the big bang onwards had to be delicately balanced if it was to produce galaxies, with perturbations neither so big that the galaxies imploded into themselves, nor so small that galaxies would not form at all. Without this fine balance, there would have been no galaxies, no stars, no planets, no life.

The distribution of gases needed to be uniform. The dispersal of even minute unevennesses (one part in 10^{40}) would have caused an alteration of temperature inhospitable to the formation of galaxies. Without this uniform distribution there would have been no galaxies, no stars, no planets, no life.

The initial heat of the big bang was so finely adjusted that it has enabled the formation of galaxies and stars. If the heat had been slightly different, we could not have now a life system based on oxygen. If things had been a little colder, there would have been insufficient turbulence for galaxies to form; and so no galaxies, no stars, no planets, no life.

The weight of neutrinos (unless they are weightless) is so finely tuned that it permits the orderly expansion of the universe and the rotation of galaxies and clusters. A very small increase in weight would mean that the universe would contract instead of expand. This contraction would mean that conditions would not be suitable for the emergence of life.

The total mass of the universe is such that it is stable, with an orderly rate of expansion and no tendency to implosion. A little more mass, and the force of gravity would have caused an implosion; a little less and the rate of expansion would not be orderly but runaway. Without this fine balance, conditions would have been too unstable to permit the evolution of life.

The whole universe as we know it depends on the existence of atoms. A minute reduction in neutron mass would probably result in no atoms at all. Without atoms no stars, no planets, no life.

A very small shift in the value of certain constants (such as the strength of the 'weak interaction' in relation to the strength of gravity, or the relation of electron mass to the mass difference between protons and neutrons) would have resulted in a different ratio of free protons to free neutrons. This would have resulted in a different proportion of helium to hydrogen in the universe. This in turn would have affected the possibility of stable stars existing. Without sufficient hydrogen, life could not have emerged on Earth.

If the force of gravity were slightly weaker, or the force of electro-magnetism slightly stronger, there would probably be no planets in the universe. If these differences were reversed, the universe would be very different from what it is. The existence of life on Earth depends on these constants.

The 'strong nuclear force' is so finely tuned that it makes possible the existence of life on Earth. Had it been a little weaker there would have been no deuterium, which is needed to enable nuclear process in the stars: had it been a little weaker, there would be little hydrogen in the universe. In either case the emergence of life on Earth would not have been possible.

A slight change in the 'weak interaction' would mean that supernovae could not have exploded, and therefore would not have produced those elements which are essential for living systems on Earth.

The interior of hot stars provides just the right temperature for the manufacture of large supplies of carbon, which is vital for living systems as we know them. Without this carbon, there would have been no life on Earth.

I have argued that the simplest explanation of what seem like extraordinary coincidences is that matter orders itself in a way that is optimal for life by the personal will of an omniscient and infinite God. I have considered other possible explanations, based on the so-called 'anthropic principle', but these seem to me to be far less probable, because they multiply possible universes which are in principle unknowable and for which there is no evidence. It is possible, of course, that the universe is the way it is because, if there were an infinite number of universes, one would be like our own; but there is no proof of, or even evidence for an ensemble of universes, and without such an ensemble, it is highly improbable that our universe could have occurred without any ultimate explanation. So it seems to me far more likely that it exists the way it does by the personal will of God.

If these 'coincidences' were to stand alone, the interpretation that I have given them would (in my judgment) be probable, but even more probable if these 'coincidences' were supported by other factors. Happily this further support is also forthcoming.

Over the last three and a half thousand million years there has been a constant climate on Earth despite the increase of 25–30 % in the sun's luminosity. Further, an atmosphere has evolved on Earth which is optimal for the existence of and maintenance of life, and it seems to have been kept constant with fine tuning by cybernetic systems which include living beings. These mechanisms also ensure the recycling of trace elements vital for life. The salinity of the oceans has also remained constant, whereas even a small increase would have made impossible the existence of living cells in the oceans.

These 'coincidences' might conceivably be a further extension of the 'anthropic principle', merely random occurrences which would have to occur or otherwise we should not be present to observe them. It seems to me, however, when I take them in conjunction with the earlier 'coincidences', far more probable that this second set of 'coincidences' also occurs because matter has an innate tendency to assemble itself in ways optimal for life, and especially for the evolution of *homo sapiens*, and that this tendency exists because God wishes beings to evolve who are capable of reflecting on themselves and on the universe which he has made, and who are able freely to enter into communion and fellowship with himself.

The evolution of living creatures, spread over billions of years, cannot adequately be summarized in a few sentences. It is possible that the whole process is random, the result of natural selection acting through random genetic mutation. Yet, when I think of all the difficulties which this hypothesis presents, it seems to me improbable. This is not merely because there is so much about the evolutionary process about which we do not know. I am not trying to introduce a 'God of the gaps'. There are too many factors (outlined in the body of the book) which militate against this solution.

There seems to be an upward trend in evolution towards the more complex forms of life. Although no clear line of development from prokariote to man can be traced, and there are many confusions and false starts, it seems (in my judgment) that matter has an innate tendency to assemble itself in more and more complex forms of life, until *homo sapiens* emerges as the end-term of that process, so far as we know it here on Earth.

Man has emerged from the hominids very rapidly, with a large increase in the size of the cortex and with a vast increase in abilities. These include his ability to speak and converse in verbal language, his mental capacities for discursive reasoning and for abstract thought. The evolution of man, with these special abilities, does not seem fully explicable on neo-Darwinian grounds. In particular his special personal qualities, including his capacity for self-awareness, self-consciousness and personal relationships cannot be explained scientifically through the complex functioning of his brain. It seems to me much more probable that human beings are made in the image of God than that they are the random product of a meaningless universe.

I am aware that a designer of the universe cannot be assumed just because we cannot attribute it solely to chance. In any case a designer is not necessarily identical with a Creator. If we are to speak meaningfully about the probability of the kind of God in whom theists believe, indications of design need to be supported by probabilities in other aspects of life.

If God exists, he is self-existent, necessary Being. If we are to regard his existence as probable, we would not merely expect him to leave his footmarks, by the act of creation and by pointers to design in the evolution of the cosmos and in the development of life. If he intends human beings to emerge from the evolutionary process who are capable of freely entering into communion and fellowship with himself, then we would expect such beings to be aware of him, and to experience the moral and aesthetic and spiritual values of which he is the source. And this is just what we do find. It seems to me far more probable that the experience of moral aesthetic and spiritual values are explained by God who is their source, rather than that they are the product of the human mind. It seems to me much more probable that the experience of conscience is due to the existence of God rather than it is merely the result of psychological mechanisms of the brain. It seems to me even more probable that religious experience which is very widely diffused is due to the existence of God rather than that it is totally based on illusion.

I must admit that I have no proof of this. Atheism remains always a possibility. But I would hold that *on the evidence atheism is wildly improbable*. It is always possible that there is no explanation of the universe — it could just be a brute fact, ultimately meaningless. It could also be that there are natural causes for the explosion of the big bang which brought space and time out of a 'singularity', even though it does not seem sensible to speak of causation operating before space and time existed. And if there are natural causes for the big bang, it could be that there is a scientific explanation of all the factors which brought it about. It is possible that the extraordinary 'coincidences' which enabled the universe to develop the way that it has are only extraordinary to us because out of an infinity of universes one was bound to turn up 'in the end' in which human beings evolved who would be capable or reflecting about it — this is possible even though by the nature of the case there can be no evidence for any universe other than our own. It is possible, in the same way, that we have the particular 'constants' in our universe that make life possible because ours is merely one of an infinite number of universes, and 'sooner or later' (only of course out of time nothing is 'sooner' or 'later') precisely these 'constants' were bound to turn up. Again it is possible that for the same reason the extraordinary cybernetic controls which have enabled life to maintain itself on the planet are the random product of a meaningless universe; almost infinitely improbable, it might appear, but among an infinity of universes and galaxies and stars and planets, bound to turn up 'in the end'. Again, you could say (and you could not be positively disproved) that the whole marvellous pageant of evolution on the planet is meaningless, totally the chance working of genetic mechanisms; or, if you agreed that matter has a tendency to assemble itself in a way that has enabled life to evolve from cell to *homo sapiens*, you could say that this is a very remarkable and extraordinary coincidence, but no more remarkable or extraordinary than the other coincidences which have been discussed, and one which would inevitably occur in an infinity of universes. You could go on to say that man's intuitions of morality and goodness and love, and his experience of moral and aesthetic values, are the random products of chemical processes in the human brain, and not a window into reality. You could add that all man's religious experience and spiritual intuitions are totally illusory. You could say that man's apparent requirement of faith in God in order to achieve his greatest potential and to meet his deepest aspirations and personal needs, is merely a psychological quirk. You could finally conclude that out of sheer coincidence all these factors have come together in human existence and there is no God.

In my judgment the convergence of all these factors makes it far, far more probable that God does exist than that he does not.

F. R. Tennant made this point about convergence many years ago when he wrote:

Causal explanation and teleological explanation are not mutually exclusive alternatives; and neither can perform the function of the other. It is rather when these several fields of fact are no longer considered one by one, but as parts of a whole, or terms of a continuous series, and when for their dovetailing and interconnectedness a sufficient ground is sought, such as mechanical and proximate causation no longer seems to apply, that divine design is forcibly suggested. Paley's watch is no analogue of the human eye; but it may none the less be an approximate analogue of nature as a whole.[1]

I am aware that, when it comes to a judgment of probabilities, it is likely that each of us is influenced by his presumptions and presuppositions, and I have written this book as a believing Christian. I have stated them, however, as fairly as I can; and I am truly perplexed that – if I have stated the case correctly – others should not reach the same judgment.

What conclusions follow from such a judgment? Pascal suggested that the mere *possibility* of God is a sufficient basis from which to make the leap of faith. William James suggested much the same. If, however, it is not only possible but even probable that God exists, this is a positive encouragement to a person to make that leap from intellectual belief into a personal commitment and trust in God. By so doing a person becomes open to the help, grace and inspiration of God to strengthen and challenge him. If we have good grounds for holding that *homo sapiens* (or if not *homo sapiens*, a creature of intelligence and moral sense, capable of personal relations with his fellow-humans and with God) is the goal to which this vast universe has been developing for billions of years, then we human beings are seized of the dignity that has been bestowed upon us in the purposes of God. If this extraordinary panorama of process and development (with all its prodigality and apparent wastefulness) has been created so that mankind (or creatures with similar qualities) can emerge, then man, as he reflects upon this, can find the self-esteem which is necessary for his well-being and without which he cannot be his true self. If man believes that he is not just the product of blind chance, he can find meaning in himself and point and purpose to his life, a worthy purpose of divine providence which is transcendent to himself and his fellowmen. He can even have hope for the future, for he no longer fears that what awaits him is as meaningless as that which brought him into being.

The probability of God has equally profound implications for the society in which man lives. At the Enlightenment the values on which society is based began a profound change. The structure of society began to be based on scientific discovery and knowledge (gained through experiment and doubt) in place of the older pre-scientific structure of society based upon faith and revelation. The high value placed on an individual person (rather than the society of which he is a member) has in the Western world led to a pluralism in which our life-style and goals become matters of personal preference, and a disintegrating society finds that it has no agreed values by which to order its common life, except perhaps the questionable basis of individual human rights (not duties) and the individual's pursuit of happiness. Nor are the socialist regimes in any better shape. Their societies are based explicitly on atheist principles, and there can be seen the same process of disintegration and cynicism. As Lesslie Newbigin has put it: 'It is significant that the only people who still cherish confidence in the future are the dissidents in each camp. The only convinced Marxists are the dissidents in the west, and the only convinced liberals are the dissidents in the east.'²

We cannot go back (nor do we wish to return) to a pre-scientific age. We are children of a scientific – indeed, a nuclear and an electronic – age. We need knowledge and experiment and doubt – but we also need faith and grace and direction. If belief in God were no longer marginalized into the privatized faith of individuals, but if it were the basic presupposition on which the whole fabric of society rests, then there would be a real possibility of society's renewal. As the agnostic Hayek has said: 'We have to make him (the individual) admit that the very things of which he has been contemptuous – these beliefs which were preserved by religion and could be preserved only be religious belief – must be recognized, even by a complete agnostic, to have been indispensable conditions of the growth of civilization.'³

Of course each generation in turn suffers from that flaw which is inherent in all humanity (and which theologians call 'original sin'), derived in part from the process out of which mankind has evolved. So the prospect can never be one of unending progress, as our Victorian forefathers erroneously thought. But if a society can combine both scientific knowledge and religious faith there can be really firm foundations for its life, not only in terms of worthy aims of justice and peace as well as prosperity, but also in terms of right relationships between people and the release of their energies and enthusiasms.

Our final question, however, concerns not the future of man

and society but the nature of the Supreme Being. Is the God of natural theology reconcilable with the God and Father of our Lord Jesus Christ? Despite all that has been written here about divine immanence, are we not left with a God more interested in process than in people, very different from the all-loving, caring, personal God who sent his Son to be the Saviour of the world?

It is true that natural theology only permits us to view God from afar. We are, as it were, out of range of his voice, too distant to recognize more than his bare outline. That is precisely why we need so badly his further self-disclosure. But it is an enormous leap forward to be able to believe, on grounds of reason and after study of the evidence, that the existence of God is very, very probable. The existence of God can never be proved; but from this firm foundation we are fully justified in making the leap of faith. Instead of a blind credulity which believes what is feared to be improbable, we can have a living faith which, on rational grounds, can be shown to be extremely probable.

Of course it is only a start. We need to learn more about this God whose footsteps are to be seen in the wonders of his creation and in the experience of mankind. Our appetite for his revelation is whetted. Our thirst for his grace is awakened. We can open our hearts to receive the revelation which he has given us; and, as we draw nearer to him, we find that he is ever present with us, and that he is indeed the God and Father of our Lord Jesus Christ in whom we can fully trust and from whom we find renewal and purpose and strength.

Instead of being somewhat downcast, wondering whether the incoming tide of scientific knowledge is sweeping away our faith, we find that, on the contrary, when we understand it aright, such knowledge serves to strengthen and confirm our inmost convictions.

Notes

Notes

1 The Possibility of Natural Theology

1. C. Bibby, *Scientist Extraordinary: the Life and Scientific Work of Thomas Henry Huxley*, Pergamon Press 1972, p. 41, cites A. Montague's Introduction to T. H. Huxley, *Man's Place in the Universe*, Michigan 1959, p. 3.

2. Cf. J. R. Moore, *The Post-Darwinian Controversies*, OUP 1979, p. 301. Douglas Spanner, in a review in *The Churchman*, 1983, p. 369, notes that Darwin's ideas on evolution were accepted most readily by those theologians who were most orthodox.

3. When I became Fellow and Dean of Gonville and Caius College, among the thirteen fellows of the College who were FRS, the majority were practising Christians or Jews. This is of course not to deny that some scientists, like Bondi, regard religion as a 'serious and habit-forming evil' (cit. P. Davies, *God and the New Physics*, Dent 1983, p. 4).

4. P. Teilhard de Chardin, *The Phenomenon of Man*, Collins 1959.

5. Cf. P. Medawar, *Pluto's Republic*, OUP 1983, p. 242.

6. Ibid., p. 249.

7. W. Temple, *Nature, Man and God*, Macmillan 1934, p. 306.

8. *Soundings* ed. A. R. Vidler, CUP 1962, p. 17.

9. Ibid., p. 3.

10. 'Dieu d'Abraham, Dieu d'Isaac, Dieu de Jacob, non des philosophes et des savants', words found at Pascal's death on a parchment sewn into his doublet.

11. S. Kierkegaad, 'Concluding Unscientific Postscript' in *A Kierkegaad Anthology* ed. R. Bretall, OUP 1947, pp. 210 ff.

12. Private correspondence.

13. Ibid.

14. Temple, op. cit., p. 520.

15. In Karl Barth, *Natural Theology* intro. J. Baillie, Bles 1946, pp. 70–128.

16. K. Barth, *The Knowledge of God and the Service of God*, Hodder 1928, p. 5.

17. J. Macquarrie, *In Search of Deity*, SCM Press 1984, p. 225.

18. A. Hardy, *The Divine Flame*, Collins 1966, pp. 198–218.

19. J. H. Newman, *The Grammar of Assent* (1870), edition published by Image Books, NY 1955, p. 227.

20. Private correspondence.

21. Private correspondence.

22. Hardy, op. cit., p. 212.

23. R. Sheldrake, *A New Science of Life*, Blond & Briggs 1981, p. 199.

2 The Beginning of Everything

1. F. Crick, *Life Itself*, Simon and Schuster, NY 1981, pp. 21f.

2. Ibid., p. 25.

3. P. C. Davies, *The Accidental Universe*, CUP 1982, pp. 90f.

4. P. C. Davies, *God and the New Physics*, Dent 1983, p. 21.

5. J. Gribbin, 'Precise measurements of nothing pins down the universe', *New Scientist*, vol. 100, 15 Dec. 1983, p. 815.

6. J. Narlikar, 'Was there a big bang?', *New Scientist* 2 July 1981, pp. 19f.

7. O. R. Jones, 'Philosophical Reflections on Creation', *Science and Religion* ed. I. G. Barbour, SCM Press 1968, p. 235.

8. J. S. Whale, *Christian Doctrine*, CUP 1941, p. 32.

9. G. Aulen, *The Faith of the Christian Church*, SCM Press 1954, p. 181.

10. R. Bultmann, *Primitive Christianity*, Meridian Books, NY 1956, p. 15, cit. O. R. Jones, art. cit.

11. P. C. Davies, *God and the New Physics*, p. 42.

12. Ibid., p. 40.

13. P. W. Atkins, *The Creation*, W. H. Freeman 1981, pp. 105f.

14. I am indebted here to A. H. Guth and P. J. Steinhardt, 'The Inflationary Universe', *Scientific American*, May 1984, p. 128. However as yet this is only 'an outline of the complete theory that physicists might one day develop' (J. Gribbin, 'One step on from the moment of creation', *New Scientist*, vol. 103, 9 Aug. 1984, p. 30).

15. E. T. Tryon, 'What made the World?', *New Scientist*, vol. 102, 8 March 1984, p. 16.

16. R. Kolb cited by J. Trevil, 'The Accidental Universe', *Science Digest*, vol. 92, no. 6, June 1984, p. 100.

17. Stephen Hawking, for example, writes about a proposal that space and time together may form a closed four-dimensional surface without boundary or edge. 'This would mean that the Universe was completely self-contained and did not require boundary conditions . . . The quantity we measure as time had a beginning but this does not mean that space-time had an edge.' Dr Hawking admits that this can only be a *proposal* which cannot be deduced but which can only be checked out against observations (cf. S. Hawking, 'The edge of spacetime', *New*

Scientist, vol. 103, 16 Aug. 1984, p. 14).

18. Michael Goulder and John Hick, *Why Believe in God?*, SCM Press 1983, p. 99.

19. R. Swinburne, *The Existence of God*, OUP 1979, pp. 131f.

20. K. Ward, *Rational Theology and the Creativity of God*, Pilgrim Press, NY 1982, p. 93.

21. R. Swinburne, op. cit., p. 102.

22. K. Ward, op. cit., p. 86.

23. Ibid., p. 109.

3   The Development of the Cosmos

1. Steven Weinberg, *The First Three Minutes of the Universe*, Deutsch 1977.

2. E.g. P. C. Davies, 'Chance or choice: is the universe an accident?', *New Scientist*, vol. 80, 16 Nov. 1978, pp. 506f; 'The Tailor-Made Universe', *The Sciences*, New York, May/June 1978, p. 6; *Other Worlds*, Dent 1980; *The Accidental Universe*, CUP 1982; *God and the New Physics*, Dent 1983.

3. P. C. Davies, *The Accidental Universe*, p. 97.

4. A. H. Guth and P. J. Steinhardt, 'The Inflationary Universe', art. cit.

5. P. C. Davies, 'The Eleven Dimensions of Reality', *New Scientist*, vol. 101, 9 Feb. 1984, p. 31; cf. M. Rees, 'Close Encounters with Eleven Dimensional Time', *The Listener*, 8 March 1984, p. 10.

6. Brandon Carter, 'Large Number Coincidences and the Anthropic Principle in Cosmology', *Confrontation of Cosmological Theories with Observational Data* (Symposium 63) ed. M. S. Longair, Dordrecht/ Boston 1974, pp. 291ff.

7. Ibid., p. 293.

8. Ibid., p. 294.

9. Stephen Hawking in *Confrontation of Cosmological Theories with Observational Data*, pp. 285f.

10. E. R. Harrison, *Cosmology*, CUP 1981, p. 113.

11. B. J. Carr and M. L. Rees, 'The Anthropic Principle and the Structure of the Physical World', *Nature*, vol. 278, p. 612.

12. M. Rees, 'Our Universe – and others', *New Scientist*, vol. 89, 29 Jan. 1981, p. 273.

13. M. Rees, 'Close Encounters with Eleven Dimensional Time', art. cit.

14. Ernan McMullin, 'How should cosmology relate to theology?', *The Sciences and Theology in the Twentieth Century* ed. A. R. Peacocke, Oriel Press 1982, p. 43.

15. It was suggested by Ludwig Botlzmann at the end of the nineteenth century.

16. 'The idea that gravity is getting weaker as the Universe ages has received a knock from a new study of the orbits of the Earth and Mars.

The results are particularly significant because they are reported by a team which includes Vittorio Canuto' (J. Gribbin, 'Gravity does not vary with Time', *New Scientist*, vol. 100, 17 Nov. 1983, p. 494). 'Results from an experiment in a salt mine 600m below ground in Ohio have extended the known life time of the proton by a factor of 10. While it is reassuring to most people to learn that the basic building block of our bodies and the world we inhabit is more nearly permanent than we knew before, the latest data may provide problems for some theorists' ('Protons live longer than theories', *New Scientist*, vol. 97, 3 Feb. 1983, p. 304).

17. J. Gribbin, *Genesis*, Dent 1981, p. 308.

18. Private correspondence.

19. P. C. Davies, *God and the New Physics*, p. 173.

20. A. R. Peacocke, *Creation and the World of Science*, OUP 1979, p. 70. See also D. J. Bartholomew, *God of Chance*, SCM Press 1984.

21. Brandon Carter, 'Large Number Coincidences and the Anthropic Principle in Cosmology', art. cit., p. 291.

22. S. Weinberg, *The First Three Minutes*, pp. 154f.

23. E. R. Harrison, op. cit., p. 113.

24. W. H. Thorpe, *Purpose in a World of Chance*, OUP 1978, pp. 11f.

4 The Atmosphere and the Oceans

1. James Jeans, *The Mysterious Universe*, CUP 1930.

2. Fred Hoyle, *The Nature of the Universe*, Blackwell 1950.

3. J. Lovelock, *Gaia: a New Look at Life on Earth*, OUP 1979.

4. Hugh Montefiore, *The Question Mark*, Collins 1969.

5. Hugh Montefiore (ed.), *Man and Nature*, Collins 1975.

6. J. Lovelock, op. cit., p. ix.

7. Ibid., p. 19.

8. Ibid., p. 10.

9. Cf. J. Gribbin, 'Carbon dioxide, ammonia – and life', *New Scientist*, vol. 94, 13 May 1982, pp. 413f.

10. J. C. J. Walker, P. B. Hays and J. F. Kasting cited by J. Lovelock in 'Gaia as seen through the atmosphere', *Biomineralization and Biological Metal Accumulation* ed. P. Westbrook and E. W. de Jong, Dordrecht/Boston 1983, p. 23.

11. Ibid., p. 23.

12. J. Lovelock, *Gaia*, pp. 31f.

13. Ibid., p. 71.

14. Ibid., p. 74.

15. Ibid., p. 85.

16. Ibid., p. 89.

17. Michael Whitfield, 'The salt sea – accident or design?', *New Scientist*, vol. 94, 11 April. 1982, p. 17.

18. J. Gribbin, *Genesis*, p. 306.

19. J. Lovelock, 'Gaia as seen through the atmosphere', p. 15.

20. J. Gribbin, op. cit., p. 306.

21. Private correspondence.

22. Cf. A. R. Peacocke, *Creation and the World of Science*, pp. 97ff.

23. Private correspondence.

24. Professor Lovelock writes further: 'It is ten years since *Gaia* was written; this is a long time in science and the subject has moved on. There is nothing you have quoted that I would wish to withdraw, but the second book I hope I can soon start on, will be a lot less speculative; indeed some of the nations have taken firm root and are now flourishing.' Dr Lovelock also points out the theory of a leading American geologist that there could be no plate techtonics on earth without the biological production of limestone (D. L. Anderson, 'The earth as a planet: Paradigms and paradoxes', *Science*, vol. 223, 1984, pp. 347–355).

5   The Emergence of Life

1. F. Crick, *Life Itself*, pp. 15f.

2. Cf. F. Hoyle and N. C. Wickramasinghe *Lifecloud*, Dent 1979.

3. F. Hoyle and N. C. Wickramasinghe, 'Where microbes boldly went', *New Scientist*, vol. 91, 13 Aug. 1981, pp. 412ff.

4. F. Hoyle, *The Intelligent Universe*, Michael Joseph 1983, p. 12.

5. F. Hoyle and N. Wickramasinghe, *Evolution from Space*, Dent 1981, p. 26.

6. F. Hoyle, *The Intelligent Universe*, p. 225.

7. *The Times*, 15 December 1981.

8. *The Times*, 21 December 1981.

9. P. Schuster, 'Prebiotic evolution', *Biochemical Evolution* ed. H. Gutfreund, CUP 1931, p. 79.

10. M. Eigen, 'The Self-Organization of Matter and the Evolution of Biological Macromolecules', *Naturwissenschaften*, 1971, p. 519, cited by A. Peacocke, *Creation and the World of Science*, p. 103.

11. Crick, op. cit., p. 56.

12. L. Orgel, 'Darwinism at the very beginning of life', *New Scientist*, vol. 94, 15 April 1982, pp. 150f.

13. Crick, op. cit., p. 88.

14. R. Sheldrake *A New Science of Life*, p. 25.

15. Ibid., pp. 25f.

16. W. H. Thorpe, *Purpose in a World of Chance*, p. 21.

17. K. K. Rao, D. O. Hall and R. Cammack, 'The photosynthetic apparatus', *Biochemical Evolution* ed. H. Gutfreund, CUP 1981, pp. 150ff.

18. G. Rattray Taylor, *The Great Evolution Mystery*, Secker & Warburg 1983, p. 207.

19. C. H. Waddington, *Principles and Problems of Development and*

Differentiation, Collier-Macmillan 1966, p. 6.

20. Private correspondence.

21. G. Rattray Taylor, op. cit., pp. 95f. The adverse reviews of the book were in *The Biologist*, vol. 6, April 1984, pp. 120ff.

22. Ibid., p. 97.

23. Cf. J. W. Valentine, 'The Evolution of Multicellular Plants and Animals' in *The Fossil Record and Evolution*, San Francisco 1982, for a succinct account.

6   *The Evolution of Species*

1. P. J. Bowler, *The Eclipse of Darwinism*, Baltimore 1983, p. 7.

2. G. Rattray Taylor, *The Great Evolution Mystery*, p. 36.

3. Mary Hesse, 'Cosmology as Myth', *Concilium*, June 1983, p. 51.

4. W. Temple, *Nature Man and God*, p. 288.

5. F. Hoyle, *The Intelligent Universe*, p. 26.

6. J. Pelikan, 'Emanation, Evolution and Development' in *Darwin's Legacy* ed. C. L. Hamrun, Harper & Row 1984, pp. 76f.

7. L. Gilkey, 'Evolution and the Doctrine of Creation', in *Science and Religion* ed. I. Barbour, SCM Press 1968, p. 165.

8. J. R. Moore, *The Post-Darwinian Controversies*, p. 239.

9. C. E. Raven, *Natural Religion and Christian Theology*, CUP 1953, vol. 1, p. 179.

10. Mary Hesse, art. cit., p. 51.

11. Ibid., p. 54.

12. Cited by John Little, 'Evolution: myth, metaphysics or science?' *New Scientist*, vol. 87, 4 Sept. 1980, p. 709.

13. G. Rattray Taylor, op. cit., p. 34.

14. Ibid., p. 154.

15. Cited by B. Halstead, 'Popper: good philosophy, bad science?', *New Scientist*, vol. 87, 17 July 1980, p. 215.

16. P. B. and J. S. Medawar, *The Life Science*, Wildwood House 1977, p. 43.

17. E. Steele, *Somatic Selection and Adaptive Evolution*, Toronto 1979. Cf. C. Judge, 'Lamarck lives – in the immune system', *New Scientist*, vol. 89, 19 Feb. 1981, pp. 483ff; M. Robertson, 'Lamarck revisited: the debate goes on', *New Scientist*, vol. 90, 23 April. 1981, pp. 230ff.

18. Medawar, op. cit., p. 43.

19. In particular Arthur Koestler, *The Ghost in the Machine*, Hutchinson 1967.

20. I am grateful for these references to G. Rattray Taylor, op. cit., pp. 149ff.

21. Science Report, *The Times*, 19 December 1983.

22. 'Hormones that go to the head', *New Scientist*, vol. 96, 2 December 1982, p. 543.

23. W. H. Thorpe, *Purpose in the World of Chance*, p. 50.
24. A. Hardy, *The Living Stream*, Collins 1965, p. 225.
25. W. H. Thorpe, *Biology and the Nature of Man*, OUP 1962.
26. Lamarck's main propositions were as follows:

1. 'That every considerable and sustained change in the surrounding of any animal involves a real change in its needs.
2. That any change of needs involves the necessity of changed action in order to satisfy those changed needs, and, in consequence, new habits.
3. It follows that such and such parts, formerly less used, are now more frequently employed and in consequence become more fully developed. New parts also become insensibly evolved by the creature by its own efforts from within.'

P. T. Saunders and W. M. Ho develop a form of neo-Lamarckism in 'Beyond neo-Darwinism – An Epigenetic Approach to Evolution', *Journal of Theoretical Biology*, 78, 1979, pp. 573–591 from which the above quotation is taken.

27. A. Hardy, op. cit., pp. 153–9.
28. R. Dunbar, 'Farming Fit for Animals', *New Scientist*, vol. 101, 22 March 1984, pp. 12f.
29. C. E. Raven, op. cit., vol. 2, p. 139.
30. Cf. 'Birds are born with a magnetic compass', *New Scientist*, vol. 101, 29 March 1984, p. 22.
31. M. Collins, 'The Importance of Being a Bugga-Bug', *New Scientist*, vol. 94, 24 June 1982, pp. 834ff.
32. Philip Morrison, 'Termites and Telescopes', *The Listener*, 23 August 1979, p. 235.
33. Private correspondence.
34. S. J. Gould, 'Punctuated equilibrium – a different way of seeing', *New Scientist*, vol. 94, 15 April 1982, p. 138.
35. C. E. Raven, op. cit., p. 136.
36. W. Paley, *Natural Theology*, Nelson 1850.
37. Private correspondence.
38. G. Rattray Taylor, op. cit., p. 61. P. Harvey and T. Clutton-Brock, however, believe that it is wrong to dismiss allometry as non-adaptive. Cf. 'The survival of the theory', *New Scientist*, vol. 98, 5 May 1983, pp. 312ff.
39. M. Ridley, 'How the Peacock Got its Tail', *New Scientist*, vol. 91, 1 Aug. 1981, p. 398.
40. A. Hardy, op. cit., p. 233.
41. G. Rattray Taylor, op. cit., p. 177.
42. A. Koestler, *The Ghost in the Machine*, p. 163.
43. Cf. D. Mackenzie, 'Why is a hand not a foot?', *New Scientist*, vol. 96, 2 Dec. 1982, pp. 558ff.
44. Cf. D. Mackenzie, 'The electricity that shapes our ends', *New*

Scientist, vol. 93, 28 Jan. 1982, pp. 217f.

45. C. H. Waddington, *Principals and Problems of Development and Differentiation*, p. 110.

46. Cf. A. Hardy, op. cit., pp. 221f.

47. A. Peacocke, op. cit., p. 95.

48. J. S. Habgood, *A Working Faith*, DLT 1980, pp. 18f.

49. P. B. and J. S. Medawar, op. cit., p. 168.

50. G. Rattray Taylor, op. cit., p. 236.

51. R. Leakey, 'The Making of Mankind', *The Listener*, 7 May 1981, p. 600.

7   The Evolution of Man

1. E. Morgan, *The Descent of Woman*, Souvenir Press 1972, p. 30. Cf. E. Morgan, 'The Aquatic Hypothesis', *New Scientist*, vol. 102, 12 April 1984, pp. 11ff.

2. W. le Gros Clark in *The Advancement of Science*, Sept. 1961, quoted by A. Koestler *The Ghost in the Machine*, p. 272.

3. C. J. Herrick, *The Evolution of Human Nature*, New York, 1961, p. 316.

4. N. Osborne, 'The Brain's Information Technology', *New Scientist*, vol. 98, 19 May 1983, p. 445.

5. R. Passingham, 'Why chimpanzees are not people', *New Scientist*, vol. 96, 4 Nov. 1982, p. 288.

6. Ibid., p. 289.

7. D. E. Wooldridge, *The Machinery of the Brain*, McGraw Hill, NY 1963, p. 18.

8. E. W. Kent, *The Brains of Men and Machines*, New York 1980, p. 142.

9. Ibid., p. 21.

10. R. Sheldrake, *A New Science of Life*, p. 203.

11. E. W. Kent, op. cit., p. 20.

12. J. Cronly-Dillon, 'The Experience that shapes our brains', *New Scientist*, vol. 96, 11 Nov. 1982, p. 366.

13. G. Ferry and L. Wingerson, 'The men who decoded the brain', *New Scientist*, vol. 92, 15 Oct. 1981, p. 155.

14. D. E. Wooldridge, op. cit.

15. G. Ferry, 'Can the injured brain recover?', *New Scientist*, vol. 93, 25 Feb. 1982, p. 491.

16. J. Cook, 'A Landmark in Brain Development', *New Scientist*, vol. 81, 1 March 1979, p. 682.

17. D. M. MacKay, *Brains, Machines and Persons*, Collins 1980, p. 23.

18. D. E. Wooldridge, op. cit., p. 61.

19. Ibid., p. 164.

20. D. M. MacKay, 'Ourselves and our brains: duality without

dualism', *Psychoneuroendocrinology*, vol. 7, no. 4, 1982, p. 293.

21. This is the view held by J. Searle in his 1984 Reith Lectures (*The Listener*, 8 November 1984, p. 16).

22. Quoted by W. H. Thorpe, *Purpose in a World of Chance*, p. 94.

23. R. Swinburne, *The Existence of God*, OUP 1979, pp. 160–175.

24. J. L. Mackie, *The Miracle of Theism*, OUP 1982, p. 129.

25. J. Monod, *Chance and Necessity*, Collins 1972, p. 31.

8 Further Dialogues Concerning Natural Religion

1. David Hume, *Dialogues Concerning Natural Religion*, Part IV.

2. Ibid.

3. It will be evident to the reader that Cleanthes here, as elsewhere in the dialogue, has read Richard Swinburne's *The Existence of God*.

4. Hume, *Dialogues*, Part XII.

5. Hume, *Dialogues*, Part IX.

6. Cleanthes has evidently been reading Keith Ward's *Rational Theology and the Creativity of God*, Blackwell 1982, p. 41.

7. Immanuel Kant, *Critique of Pure Reason*, Transcendental Dialectic, Book II, Chapter 3, section vi.

8. The phrase is used, I think, for the first time by Francis Crick in *Life Itself*, pp. 89ff.

9. Philo here is evidently referring to R. Sheldrake's *A New Science of Life*.

10. J. S. Mill, 'Nature', *Collected Works of J. S. Mill* ed. J. M. Robson, Routledge, vol. 10 1969, p. 399.

11. William James, *The Varieties of Religious Experience*, Longmans 1928, p. 525. This is quoted by J. L. Mackie *The Miracle of Theism*, p. 182. Both Philo and Cleanthes appear to have some acquaintance with the latter book.

12. The sources of evidence for this statement can be found in my *Taking our Past into our Future*, Fount 1978, p. 57, note 1; A. Hardy *Darwin and the Spirit of Man*, Collins 1984, pp. 226f.

13. John Hick in Michael Goulder and John Hick, *Why Believe in God?*, p. 46.

9 The Concept of Divine Immanence

1. J. H. Newman, *Grammar of Assent*, p. 95.

2. John. V. Taylor, *The Go-Between God*, SCM Press 1972, p. 26.

3. Ibid., p. 28.

4. H. B. Swete, *The Holy Spirit in the Ancient Church*, Macmillan 1912, p. 378.

5. Julian of Norwich, *Revelations of Divine Love*, ch. 5.

6. *Polarity* (ET Oxford 1935), p. 33., cited by E. L. Mascall, *He Who Is*, Longmans 1943, p. 126.

7. J. R. Moore, *The Post-Darwinian Controversies*, pp. 337f.

8. A. R. Peacocke, *Creation and the World of Science*, p. 204. Cf. *Science and the Christian Experiment*, OUP 1973, p. 124.

9. M. Wiles, *The Remaking of Christian Doctrine*, SCM Press 1974, p. 37.

10. Ibid.

11. W. Temple, *Nature, Man and God*, p. 292.

12. L. Hodgson, *For Faith and Freedom*, Blackwell, vol. 2 1957, p. 107 (reissued in one vol., SCM Press 1968).

13. John Taylor, op. cit., p. 31.

14. L. C. Birch, 'Creation and the Creator', *Science and Religion* ed. I. G. Barbour, p. 211.

15. W. R. Matthews, *God in Christian Thought and Experience*, Nisbet 1930, pp. 200f.

16. H. Bergson, *Creative Evolution*, Macmillan 1911, p. 399.

17. L. J. Henderson, *The Fitness of the Environment*, Peter Smith, Boston 1958, p. 306.

18. H. K. Schilling, *The New Consciousness in Science and Religion*, SCM Press 1973, p. 249.

19. Cf. I. Williams, *The Beginnings of Welsh Poetry*, University of Wales Press 1972, pp. 101f. I am indebted to Canon Allchin for this reference.

20. Teilhard de Chardin, *Hymn of the Universe*, Collins 1965, p. 152.

21. *Le Milieu Divin*, Collins 1960, p. 15, n. 1; *Hymn of the Universe*, p. 28. Both these are cited by J. A. T. Robinson, *Exploration into God*, SCM Press 1967, p. 85.

22. J. A. T. Robinson, op. cit., p. 86.

23. A. Pope, *Essay on Man*, Epistle 1, ix, 279–80.

24. H. Oppenheimer, *Incarnation and Immanence*, Hodder 1973, pp. 37f.; cf. C. E. Raven, *Creator Spirit*, Hopkinson 1927, pp. 107ff.

10 The Probability of God

1. F. R. Tennant, *Philosophical Theology*, vol. ii, CUP 1930, p. 104, quoted by J. Macquarrie, *In Search of Deity*, p. 210; cf. R. Swinburne, *The Existence of God*, p. 13.

2. L. Newbigin, *The Other Side of 1984*, WCC 1983, p. 4.

3. F. Hayek, Channel 4, 19 Sept. 1984, quoted in *The Guardian*, 17 Sept. 1984.

Index of Names

Index of Names